Love to Sherand + ...

March 27, 1998

Virginia Henkins

STONEWALL'S COURIER

The Story of Charles Randolph and General Jackson

STONEWALL'S COURIER

The Story of Charles Randolph and General Jackson

by

VIRGINIA HINKINS

LOFT PRESS
FORT VALLEY, VIRGINIA

Published by Loft Press, Inc.
P.O. Box 126, Fort Valley, Virginia 22652

©1997 Virginia Hinkins

Second edition
Newly illustrated by James Steven Shell

ISBN 0-9630797-4-3

Library of Congress Catalog Card Number 97-74060

Printed and bound in the United States of America.

Acknowledgments

THERE ARE so many people who sustain an author until her book is published: the family who cooperates with hours of inaccessibility, and those who help search for the facts underlying a story such as this.

In my case, Phyllis Whitney was friend, critic and inspiration, as was Bernice Bryant.

Mr. Randolph Carter, great nephew of the hero of *Stonewall's Courier*, graciously provided many facts of the family history, took me to visit The Grove, which he rebuilt, and contacted Charley's son, Charles Randolph, to write reminiscences of his father's tales of the Civil War.

To all these, my appreciation and gratitude.

*Dedicated to the memory of
our grandson, Jack Dughi.*

Contents

1 *The Grove*

IT WAS just past dawn as Charley Randolph watched his brother gravely shake hands with Father and swing into the saddle. The light from the rising sun glinted on the gold buttons of the young officer's jacket; there was the rattle of his saber and the quick crunch of steel horseshoes on the pebbly road.

Robert paused and looked back at them, checking his prancing horse. The powerful gelding that had carried him fox hunting through the counties of Northern Virginia was now a splendid mount for the new Captain of the Black Horse Cavalry. The slaves were clustered at the door, and Silas, the farm foreman, said boastfully, "Lawdy, ain't our Massa Robert purty?"

Charley stood on the porch of The Grove with his wide mouth spread in a grin of pride. Today was the end of May 1862, but the folks of Fauquier County couldn't take seriously the bad news from the fronts. A few more months and the South's gallant young men like Robert would end the war in a blaze of glory.

I'm going with him, Charley thought. I'm sixteen. They have to stop treating me like a child.

He rushed down the steps to Robert and saluted. "I'm volunteering for your outfit," he said. "I'll get my horse right now and. . . ."

But Father grabbed his wrist. "None of that, sir! Thank God your mother didn't live to see the day your sisters had to take their little ones and refugee south. Robert must fight. You and I will stay on the farm and produce horses and food for the army—and your special duty is school."

School! Charley felt humiliated in the hearing of the slaves; old Captain Randolph was strong-willed and usually right. He turned appealingly to his brother, "It's just that I'm so short," he pleaded. "I'm sixteen now, you remember."

But Robert took off his cap with a merry flourish. "You have the hardest job, Brother Charles; I'd much rather fight the war than pass your geometry exam this morning." He wheeled the horse, swinging his cap in a wide arc that included all The Grove. "Goodbye."

There was an answering shout from the slaves and Father watched Robert gallop his hunter down the road to Warrenton with only a wordless salute, too deeply moved to speak.

"Father, the war will be over if you don't let me go soon," Charley burst out. "The Randolphs have always fought in wars. You did—in 1812."

Captain Randolph seemed to ignore him. "Silas," he called to the Negro foreman, "we'll mow the hay pasture by Licking Run today. Get the men started. I'll be down directly."

The man moved off towards Cabin Hill, where five log cabins stood black against the rising sun. They watched as he hurried up the hill calling, and the farm workers came from the huts, stretched, and took down their long scythes that hung in the apple tree. Closer to the "big house" were two more cabins for the in-servants, then a separate building for the kitchen, and the brick walk through the vegetable and flower gardens to the main house. The residence of the nineteen-hundred-acre farm was not a mansion, but a two-story rectangle of stone built directly into the hillside. There was no excess of luxury here; it was the home of a good husbandman that seemed to rise, like his crops, from the fertile earth.

"You know, Charles," Captain Randolph said, watching as one of the slaves dawdled sullenly behind Silas and the other workers, "when Cousin Robert Lee was a little tyke he used to visit here and around with his nearby kinfolks. For a time he went to the same school building you'll use this morning." Charley's father looked down at him with a grim face. "Yes sir. We Randolphs have always fought for what we believed was right—even to becoming General of the Armies of Virginia. But none of us, sir, has failed in school. Are you going to be the first to give us a reputation for being dull-witted?"

"But I'm not dull-witted!" Charley answered furiously. "I'm not!"

11

"Of course you're not. You're too caught up in playing at soldiering. If necessary, I shall take away your pony and pistols until you've recollected yourself sufficiently to pass the examination. You have several hours before the schoolmaster comes. I suggest you go now and study." The Captain strode toward the stable but turned to add, "Good luck, my son."

Charley was too angry to answer. It was because he was so small that they treated him like a child. "Playing at soldiering." His father's words galled him worse than a saddle burn. Charley Randolph was going to be one of the greatest cavalry officers in the South. But how could he unless he spent hours on his pony with pistols and rusty saber fighting practice battles? Could he help it if his eyes closed as automatically as the book opened when he sat down to study at the end of the day? He could hardly expect to pass the re-exam this morning. But Father would never let up until the thing was done. He sighed and started toward the house to find the hateful geometry book.

Black Sadie was carrying a tray of breakfast dishes from the house to the kitchen. He heard her say, "Unc Ben, you see how bad po' little Massa Charley want to go to wah? Ain't that a sight? I told Miss Bess, fo' she left, that I could fix him a potion that'd make him grow as big as Massa Robert. Miss Bess, she got pow'ful mad—she say she better not hear of me feedin' her brother none of my witch's brew. She say to pray to the Lawd to keep him safe, dat's all."

Unc Ben's woolly white head nodded with the rhythm of his hoe. "Amen, Sadie, amen. But it don't look like he ever gonna grow big like the rest of the fambly."

Sadie tee-heed shrilly. "Yas suh, they's a runt in every litter, ain't it so, Unc Ben?"

Charley turned abruptly from the house and ran down the road. It was about a mile to the one-room school on his uncle's farm where he and his numerous cousins and kin were taught their lessons. Runt of the litter, was he? Charley raced at top speed. "Bet I can out-ride and out-shoot any of them. . . ." Barging through the door, he grabbed up the yardstick that always hung by a nail behind the master's desk. Charley measured himself, heaving for breath. Five feet two inches tall! Stupid Sadie didn't know that the ideal cavalryman was just five feet five—only three inches more was all he wanted to grow. Maybe he hadn't grown last year so he'd grow an extra amount this year. The idea wasn't smart, but it was comforting.

He dropped onto a pine bench, looking dully around; the only light came through high fanlight windows well above eye level. The walls were hung with steel engravings: the Parthenon, George Washington, Napoleon of France. Charley stared at Napoleon's picture—Napoleon had been a little man too. On the shelves and even on the floor were stacks of dusty books that looked as if they hadn't been disturbed for a generation. The room was heavy with the oppressive quiet of a deserted place; the older boys had joined the army, the girls and younger boys had refugeed south of Richmond. The few pupils left had completed their school term—all except Charley.

Opening the textbook, he settled down with a sigh. "The square of the hypotenuse . . . the daggoned square of the plug-ugly hypotenuse."

The next hour went slowly, with the bobwhite's whistle reminding him how sunny and cheerful it was outside the half-open door. Then the natural humming of a May morning hushed and Charley looked up from his book. Surely the schoolmaster couldn't be coming already.

"All right," said a low voice. "Here's a good enough place. Nobody'll see us behind this building." There was a muttered reply.

What was this all about? Charley got up and moved stealthily to the back of the room. He pressed his ear against the wall.

"You gonna get me them hosses or ain't you?" the first voice demanded. It was a southerner's drawl but there was nothing soft about it. This was a stranger.

"How much is he wuth? The ol' Cap'n best 'un—that big ches'nut he call Sun Bolt?" Charley recognized the voice of his father's stableboy.

"Ah, that one," the stranger said with relish. "Enough to buy your freedom, that's how much, black boy."

There was a moment's silence. "I—I jus' don't know. The ol' Cap'n—he say he ain't gonna let nobody come down from the no'th and fo'ce him to do nuttin—but when the wah is over, he give us our free papers. . . ."

The white man laughed. "You fool—he ain't gonna do any such thing."

"Yas he is. Ol' Cap'n, he work hard and work his people hard too, but when he give his word, Mistuh, thas all a body needs." He paused. "Will you sell Sun Bolt to the Yankees?"

"I'll sell him wherever I get the most Union money—no Confederate paper for me. Why don't you get smart? There ain't going to be nothing left in this country but mules and plow horses when I'm through."

"Traitor! Robber!" Charley muttered. Quietly he carried over a bench and placed it under the window, climbed up and strained to see through the glass. But he still wasn't high enough to look down on the two men. The thick old books stacked on the floor would raise him farther and this might be his only chance to see the traitor's face. Charley moved quickly, and in his haste a handful of yellowed scraps of paper slid from the biggest volume and fluttered to the floor. Stacking books on the bench, he peered down at the two.

"Tomorrow then. Remember, if you don't get the money for that hoss, someone else will." The white man was big, rawboned, with squinty eyes. He looked like one of the door-to-door peddlers that had lately become sut-

15

lers, following the army camps with high-priced goods. They were a new type in this country, but one saw them frequently in Warrenton now that both armies were only forty miles away. He watched the man lope down the road, and the stableboy scuttled away in another direction.

Charley jumped down from the stack. Imagine that stranger laying his heavy hands on Sun Bolt—Sun Bolt, the magnificent thoroughbred hunter they were saving as a remount for Robert. Such a horse was the very spirit of victory; the enemy could *not* have him. He, Charles Randolph, would see to that.

But how? Warn Father and catch these two, but what about the others strangers in town and the sullen slave they'd noticed this morning? The same pattern would be repeated over and over. Sun Bolt wouldn't be safe until he was in Robert's outfit with a Confederate brand on his slick hide. Charley felt a tingling sensation creep up his back—hadn't he better ride Sun Bolt to Robert? Hadn't he better stay and join up?

He glanced around excitedly, noticing the opened geometry book and the scraps of old paper on the floor. Should he or not? Distractedly, he replaced the bench and books and gathered up the fallen papers.

The large scrawl of a child's labored handwriting caught his attention and he held up the script to the light. "Robert Lee," he read incredulously. It was a one-sentence copybook epigram, the letters carefully correct, "A

foe may give lessons in fighting, but life teaches learning,"
signed, Robert Lee.

Charley gasped; this was it—fight—this was his answer.
He'd heard Father roar, "Poppycock!" whenever the Ne-
groes spoke of signs.   But the old Captain had never seen
a sign so obvious.   To Charley this was a personal order
from General Robert E. Lee.

Folding the little scrap of paper, he carefully placed it
in his breast pocket.   He slapped shut the geometry book
and ran toward the door.   Charles Randolph was taking
Sun Bolt to his army's lines; he'd join and ride the great
horse to victory himself.   That is, if Robert didn't need
him.

At the door, Charley hesitated, turned and saluted the
picture of Napoleon—then raced for The Grove.

2 Sun Bolt

CHARLEY finished writing his note and read it over:

Dear Father,

I'm taking Sun Bolt to Robert and I'll join up. You won't be angry when I'm famous.

I heard a stranger trying to bribe a slave to steal Sun Bolt and the other good horses to sell to the Yankees. The stranger was big, with squinty eyes and a rough accent. You ought to catch the traitor.

> Respectfully,
> Your son,
> Charles

Now, where to hide the note so that Father would find it—not Sadie, and not too soon? Charley went into his father's room and placed it under the candleholder on the bed table; he covered the corner that still showed with the Bible. Captain Randolph held vesper services for the household every evening after supper—he'd find the note then.

Back in his own room, Charley pocketed the money his grown sister had given him "in case of an emergency."

Surely she would agree that this was it. He took his derringer pistols from their case, hefted them lovingly in the
palms of his hands, and thrust them under his belt. They
were small, so small that he could easily have hidden the
two under his shirt. He snatched up the powder flask,
jammed his pockets full of balls and caps, and strapped the
rusty saber to his side. As a last thought, he slung over his
shoulder an old canteen of Robert's, with the letters C.S.A.
stamped across it. He clanked out of the house and
walked to the stable, outwardly unconcerned but inwardly
going hot and cold with excitement.

No one called. No one seemed to notice as they went
about the daily chores. Charley stepped inside the stable
door, took down Sun Bolt's bridle from its peg and hurried into the box stall.

Sun Bolt threw up his head in alarm; an odd blaze from
poll to nose streaked his face and gave him his name. The
boy looked up at the big horse—he couldn't begin to
reach Sun Bolt's head to slip on the bridle. If he climbed
on the manger, all his clanking equipment would send his
mount shying to the other side of the stall.

"Eeeas-y, boy, eea-sy," Charley crooned. He stood beside the horse and ran his hand soothingly down the silken
neck. The flesh twitched away from his touch and the
horse's feet shifted nervously in the bedding. Then
slowly, Sun Bolt quieted, snorting and looking down curiously.

"That's right—lower your head a little more. Eea-sy."

At last, Charley flipped the reins over the horse's neck. Something moved behind him and he turned to see the stableboy watching him—the slave who had secretly met the traitor.

"Massa Charley—let me saddle yo' pony for you." Obediah was a couple of years older than Charley and a good deal heavier. "I ain't had time to curry this 'un yet. Been pow'ful busy this mawnin'."

"Yes, I know," Charley answered meaningfully, secure with the derringers pressing against his body. "But I think I'll take Sun Bolt this time."

"Yo' pappy say for me not to let you ride this hoss—he's too big a hoss for anybody but a full-growed man." Obediah's manner was sullen.

"I am a grown man," Charley said, anger prickling through him. "I didn't tell Father it was you with that horse thief this morning. I won't, but I heard you."

Obediah looked startled and his fists clenched. Charley tried to stand big under the frowning gaze. He knew his artillery was just in the way since he could never draw a weapon on Obediah. The Negro lowered his gaze. "You done me a favor. Guess I better hep you saddle up."

After that, Charley was quickly mounted. "I'm going for a long ride, but you won't tell anyone until you have to, will you, Obediah?"

The stableboy understood. "No suh. But you knows that hoss is too much for you, Massa Charley. You'll need a boy to take keer of you."

"No, I won't." Charley sat proudly in the saddle as

Sun Bolt pranced in a tight circle. "You take care to stay out of trouble yourself. I can ride any horse in Fauquier County, including this one." He let Sun Bolt step out towards the road to Warrenton. "Remember, don't tell. Goodbye."

Charley didn't even glance behind him, but strained all his attention forward to the Shenandoah Valley and war. Forty miles with a horse like Sun Bolt would be easy. He made as good time as he dared, being careful not to give the impression of undue haste as he rode past the neighbors' farms and the townspeople in Warrenton. He stopped briefly at the courthouse square and called to the town loafer who lounged in the shade.

"Hey, Lute, what's the news from the Valley today?"

Lute shook his head. "Seems like they're up the Valley one day and down the next—like a hog what sees two cornfields and can't make up his mind. . . ."

"I know," Charley interrupted, "but have you heard anything this morning?"

"Feller 'round here a while back said Jackson's in Winchester comin' down the Valley like a fox runnin' for his den—Yankees is trying to catch him—comin' in from every which way." Lute guffawed loudly. "You better ride home, son. Yankees see you dressed up like that, they're liable to think you belong to the army."

Charley grinned. "Yes sir, they just might at that." He wheeled Sun Bolt in the road and trotted away with a flourish—straight for the Valley.

Once beyond the territory where he was known, Charley

began to loosen the tight rein he held on his horse. On the thirty-first of May in '62, summer had already set in, hot and brooding. Sun Bolt's feet pounded the baked road hollowly, and red dust stuck to the places where the sweat trickled down his legs. They went quickly through the pine thickets, past the green pastures, closer to the Blue Ridge, biggest barrier to the Valley. The mountains were always blue-gray, Charley reflected, just as the Shenandoah River water was always green. They climbed over the mountain by the winding road, and down again until Charley caught a glimpse of the rolling Shenandoah through the foliage. He began to sing,

"Oh, Shenandoah, I hear you calling. . . ."

Again on level ground, he chose a road that would bring him south of Winchester to the town of Front Royal. From there he could quickly find Jackson's forces. And Sun Bolt was just his style, powerful and eager; no more bobbing along on a pony for him.

For the first time, he dared to urge Sun Bolt and the horse responded like a hound on the scent. They raced down the road, their sweat mingling, their two bodies moving as one. Charley rode with the expertness of a bird coasting before a March wind, shifting, balancing, always in easy control.

Exaltation welled up in his throat until it burst from his lips in a yell. "Yaaaa—ee—ha—ahhhh."

"Charge," he screamed, leaning over to unsheathe his

saber, while imitating the wild call of the bugle. Around the bend in the road they thundered, to come up abruptly behind three horsemen plodding along in the heat.

"Whoa—now, whoa," Charley pulled on the reins and stared in amazement. Up a few yards was another little group of men and all of them wore blue uniforms. The enemy on this side of Front Royal?

Sun Bolt shook his head and seemed annoyed by Charley hauling on his bit, but his charge did not falter. They swept down the road, indifferent to the six horsemen in the way. Charley still held his saber over his head, the way he'd drawn it a few moments before when "playing at war." The first three soldiers scattered to the side of the road, amid startled cries and scuffling hooves. The second group whirled and prepared to meet the attack. Charley flailed with his saber as he passed through the men, thrusting and parrying as he had practiced without really seeing his foe. Nothing came in contact with him, but his vigor was so great that the weapon flew out of his hand and fell clattering to the road. Then, he was in front of the six horsemen and they were racing after him, shots cracking above the rumble of hooves.

The sound of shooting did something to Sun Bolt—if he was running away before, he was running wild now. Over a stone fence, through the young corn blades, over another stone wall into the tall wheat; a broad jump across a swampy creek; up and over into a barnyard where pigs and fowl scattered in every direction. Then out again—

now down a farm lane, now swerving and ducking through a wooded area with no path at all, then on the main road again and off across country on the other side.

"You won't throw me—you won't," Charley muttered. What had been fun was now an endurance test. The shooting, when he remembered it, had long since faded away. Sun Bolt galloped on until miles later he seemed content to let Charley control him.

By late afternoon, they stood on a ridge overlooking Front Royal. Charley moved cautiously, not sure whose forces occupied the tiny town. According to the news along the way, the Yankees had been close once today— later on, the Rebs. He was smeared with dust and sweat, had thrown away his empty saber sheath and drained the battered canteen. Pangs of hunger pinched his stomach and urged him towards the store where he could buy corn meal, molasses and a slab of bacon.

At first, the town seemed deserted. The houses looked severe along the road with doors closed and blinds pulled. Obviously a knock on the door would not be answered. A little girl peeped out at him from behind a stack of cooking-stove wood on her front porch.

"Hey," he called, "where is everybody?"

"I don't know," the child answered, already understanding something of war. "Are you a soldier?"

"Of course." Charley swung around his canteen with the letters C.S.A. for her to see. "Any Yankees in town?"

The little girl smiled at him. "No—they were only

over there," she said, pointing towards the Massanutten Mountains. "They've gone. You'd better hurry if you want to catch up."

"Yes ma'am." Charley bowed from the saddle to her, and trotted towards the inevitable crossroads store.

Some of the men of the town were gathered at the store, oldsters and gangling boys, pushed to the sidelines of war, talking about it endlessly but able to do little. A few horses were tied to the hitching rack, switching flies aimlessly. As Charley rode up, they watched him suspiciously but kept on with the heated discussion.

"Yes suh—here ran six or seven Yankees and this *one* boy from our side come up and whipped 'em all—all seven or eight of 'em. I seen it with my own eyes." The old man banged his cane on the porch floor to emphasize the point. The others agreed loudly and Charley nodded his head too. He was sure that one Reb could out-run six of them—hadn't he just done it?

"And their horses are no good," Charley broke in, still mounted and slapping Sun Bolt's magnificent neck proudly.

"Hey, Peanut, where you think you're going with a horse like that?" one of the boys called.

"I'll be dad-shamed." An angular mountaineer of fifty stepped out and scrutinized Charley and his mount. "Jist where did you git a hoss sich as that?"

"He's mine—and I'm taking him to join up with my brother Robert who's Captain of the Black Horse Cavalry." Charley sat tall in the saddle and spoke with the greatest dignity he could muster.

The whole group burst into laughter. "You in the Black Horse Cavalry. . . . He, he! My brother's name is Santa Claus—I'm figurin' on joining his reindeer outfit—he, he!" The old men slapped their thighs and pointed at Charley. The youngsters grinned.

Charley felt his face burning and he yanked a derringer from under his belt. "If you don't believe me, we can fight it out. . . ."

"Shut up!" The mountaineer seemed to take command of the group where several guns had already appeared in answer to Charley's. "Can you really ride that hoss?" he asked.

"Of course I can," Charley retorted, with mental reservations about running away. "He can never throw me."

"Well, hooo-ray. Let's see you ride him then, Genril." Shots rang out and little puffs of dust spurted up about Sun Bolt's feet.

And Charley did ride him somehow, as Sun Bolt pitched and rocked and tore up the ground. The pistol flew from his hand as Sun Bolt threw up his head and struck Charley under the chin. Then he was carried wildly down the road that led towards the main valley. Charley clung to the horse's neck, with waves of nausea making his eyes and mouth water, blood trickling from between his bitten lips.

They raced toward the Massanutten Mountains—exactly where the enemy had been in force today. Charley tried to stop Sun Bolt, but it would have been as easy for him to roll the mountain over. He felt himself slipping to one side and with a desperate effort regained his balance. There were waves of blackness now before his eyes. Once he glimpsed a rider dashing in from a side road in front of him. More blackness.

Then he realized that the horseman had grabbed Sun Bolt's bridle near the bit. He was conscious of a struggle, the spurts of speed and short stops that jerked him, the over-all lessening of the pace, and at last the runaway was stopped.

Charley felt himself slipping from the saddle again, but this time a pair of sinewy arms reached out and steadied him. He glanced up into the horseman's face and recognized the mountaineer from the Front Royal store.

"He didn't throw me," Charley mumbled. "I told you he couldn't." After that came blackness again.

3 *The Army Marches Past*

W<small>HEN CHARLEY</small> opened his eyes he was riding on the front of the saddle with the mountaineer; Sun Bolt was being led behind. They were passing through a woodland trail and Charley was careful not to betray his returned consciousness, but sagged against the horse's neck trying to figure what might happen. The mountaineer's hand held him firmly by the back of his britches and the one remaining derringer poked him in the stomach.

The horse stopped suddenly; the man sprang from the saddle and threw Charley over his shoulder like a sack of flour.

"Ooow," Charley gasped.

"Playin' possum on me, eh? I suspicioned you." The mountaineer put him on the porch of a small log cabin. "Go in and set down now; you're 'bout the color of a toad's belly. I'll be back soon's I see to the hosses. There'll be rain before morning."

Charley stepped down onto the dirt floor of the cabin and walked unsteadily to the fireplace. The room was as bare looking as a stable, as black as a smokehouse. Steel traps, hunting knives and an old musket littered the mantel—then Charley stared. As carefully placed in the center as his sister's imported vase was a cornhusk doll as old and as black as the walls around it.

After a while, the mountaineer returned with a freshly skinned rabbit and pushed a stool under Charley. "Set down, I said. I'll get us some grub. My name's Quint— Quinton Hocks. What's your'n?"

"Charles Randolph. I'm starved—haven't had anything to eat since before dawn."

"Thought as much," Quint said. "Runnin' away from home and ain't old enough yit to think further ahead than your hoss' nose."

"How'd you know?" Charley asked, startled.

"Reckon I oughta'." Quint busied himself making rabbit stew, throwing chunks of meat, potatoes and kernels of dried corn into a kettle swung over the coals. "My boy run away to the cavalry. Only chile I had. Big though, nearly twict as big as you."

"Maybe I'll see him. What's his name?" Charley moved his stool closer to the stew.

"Quint—same as mine," he said. "His maw named him fer me. She died when he was a babe."

There was a long silence while the stew bubbled in the pot. Finally Charley asked, pointing to the mantel, "Did she make the doll?"

"Yep. He never liked it though. Seems like he never took to nothing we tried to do fer him. Run away and joined a gentleman's outfit but now he hates it cause they got fine hosses and his'n is a mountain cob." Quint thrust

29

a ladle into the stew and handed Charley a tin plate. "That's why I want you to trade me your'n."

"No. I couldn't do that. I'm taking him to my brother Robert." Charley dipped from the pot hungrily.

"You'll never make it." Quint shook his head and his voice was sorrowful. "You ride like a young eagle but that hoss is too big fer you. Bet you can't even bridle him without you stand on somethin'. What you gonna stand on in an open field?"

Charley couldn't answer but continued to gulp his food. There was a lot in what the old man said. "I'll get through," he said. "Sun Bolt can out-run anything'...."

"Could this mornin' maybe," Quint interrupted, his melancholy increasing. "But tonight he's got an ankle swole bigger'n my two fists. Can't ride him fer a couple days and by that time, Jackson'll left this country to the Yankees fer a spell." He took a derringer from his hip pocket and flipped it over to Charley. "Here, you dropped your pistol. You'll likely need it bad."

Charley sat and thought about his horse. He tried to make a plan, but now that his stomach was full, there was a terrible weariness. If only he could sleep for an hour. "Can you hide Sun Bolt in the mountain until he's well again?"

"Shore. And I'll trade you the smartest ding-dong pony in the Shennydore Valley fer him—you kin ride her outa here at dawn. Is it a deal?" Quint asked urgently.

"I don't know." Charley slipped from the stool and stretched out on the hearth. He fell into a heavy sleep

30

and it seemed only an instant until something dragged him back to consciousness.

Quint was shaking his shoulder. "He's gone. That hoss done broke out of the paddock and took off up the mountain."

"What?" Charley jumped to his feet and dashed out into the rain-drenched morning. How quickly the night had gone. Shrouds of mist clung to the ground; the foliage looked black and matted together. It would be hard to find an entire army in the woods this morning.

Quint pointed to where the flimsy fence was broken apart; the paddock was empty except for a single common-looking pony. "Thar—thar's where he left. And you got no time to look fer him. I seen signal lights from mountain to mountain last night before the fog set in. I can't read their code but I know their meanin'. Jackson says to hurry."

Charley tried not to let the urgent words panic him. The rotten boards had been kicked and shattered but he figured the mountaineer's heavy boot could have done the job as well as Sun Bolt. He turned to the old man angrily. "Did you break it—did you let him out?"

"Me? Act the rascal with you?" Quinton sounded shocked. "Ain't I brung you home and tended you like a babe?"

Charley looked at the ground, ashamed.

"I'll find him when the weather clears," he continued. "I'll hide him and doctor him too. Not my fault he ain't got sense like my pony thar." He pointed to the rusty animal who stood as patiently as the forest oaks, shedding the rain in rivulets down her sides. "But I'll trade you—this 'un is crackin' smart. That 'un of yourn might be dead fer all I know. Poor tradin'." Quint shook his head dismally.

Charley knew he had been outsmarted. But what could he do? Quinton Hocks' son would ride Sun Bolt.

Half an hour later, he bobbed down the trail on Pebbles. Her name described the pony well—small, brownish, unworthy of a second glance. She trotted solemnly along through the fog and dripping foliage, taking her new master out of the mountain. Charley was forced to trust her judgment since he had only the vaguest idea of how he'd come. It was cool this morning and he shivered, half from discomfort and half in despair for Sun Bolt.

They passed quickly into more open country. Suddenly, there was scuffling from behind the brush beside the road and a sharp voice called, "Halt!"

Almost instantly two horsemen were beside him. "Who are you? What are you doing here?" Someone yanked the derringers from his belt.

After the first startled moment, a wide grin spread across Charley's face. The men were dressed in gray, and their manner and voice told him with certainty that they were from the Army of Northern Virginia. "Whew—you scared me at first. You're the men I'm looking for. Where's the Black Horse Cavalry this morning? I want to find my brother and . . . ."

32

"So you want to know where the cavalry is?" the sentry interrupted. "Well, we ain't telling you. Take him into Strasburg, Jim, and put him under guard."

Charley decided to keep his story for their commanding officer and went willingly with his captor into the main valley.

Boom—boom. Cannonading from the north. Then a steady roar from the west. And as they hastened down the road from the east, Charley guessed that his guard expected the enemy there too. Was he getting to the war just in time to be trapped?

They passed into the outskirts of Strasburg where soldiers were camping and walking in groups. Lean, hard men in homespun gray, glancing to the north—the west —the east, and moving restlessly towards a closer sound. It was the rumble and grind of wagon wheels on a macadam road; hundreds of wheels, hundreds of clopping hooves, and above it, the urgent cries of the wagoneers.

"If'n it wasn't for Jackson," one of the soldiers yelled to his buddy, "I wouldn't bet you a plug of tobacco on our chances of gettin' out of this one."

"Been out of tobacco for a week," was the reply. "But thank God for Stonewall."

There was a half-groan from the men as they came in sight of the Valley Pike, choked with supply wagons, ambulances, field forges, batteries, everything on wheels in a great army retreating steadily southward.

"Here, boy." Charley's guard jerked him from the

saddle and handed him over to another sentry. "Put him in the wagon with that feathered sutler."

"Wait—I've got to talk to your commanding officer," Charley objected, but the guard was already spurring away.

Charley told his story to the new sentry. "I'll send word. Now get in there," he said and boosted Charley into the canvas-covered wagon.

A broad-shouldered man sat cross-legged among boxes, barrels and crates and silently smoked his pipe. He wore a feathered headdress and two feathers hung from the bowl of his pipe.

"Are you an Indian chief?" Charley asked.

"Ummp," was the reply. "You got money?"

"Some. Where you from? Whose side you on?" Charley had to shout above the clatter outside the wagon.

"Ummp. Me not care. Yankee eagle catch little gray rabbit in sharp claw now."

"Is that so?" Charley yelled at him. "Nobody can catch Stonewall!"

The chief shrugged. "You got money, I got magic medicine. You buy."

"I don't want any." Charley sat down on the floor of the wagon.

"Me little man one time. Take magic medicine. Grow to biggest man in tribe. They make me chief."

Charley shrugged in his turn and sat listening to the sounds. Intermittent rain spattered on the canvas like hot fat in a frying pan. The hours crept by as painfully as the supply train; the rumbling and booming blended until he felt sure that enemy armies were closing the trap from every direction. The cold sweat popped out on his upper lip and he called out repeatedly to the sentry. Couldn't he go? Couldn't he find his brother himself?

At first the guard ignored him, but past noon his temper grew short. Ranks of prisoners tramped down the pike. Was Jackson going to leave his own brigade to be caught in the trap? Charley's barrage of questions suddenly brought a quick answer.

"Shut up," the guard yelled and slapped him across the mouth. "If'n I hear you or see you again, I'll thrash the livin' daylights out of you like your pappy shoulda done."

Charley turned his back on the chief who silently watched and listened. The cut in his lip that Sun Bolt had made was opened afresh but he didn't mind that nearly so much as the threat to thrash him like a child. If only the guard had offered to shoot him like a man. If only he hadn't been too small for Sun Bolt. If only he'd just grow three more inches. . . .

"All right, Chief—I'll buy your magic medicine."

The Indian put his hand into a box and brought out a small bottle.

Charley counted out the money, grabbed the medicine and took a quick searing gulp.

"Another bottle?" Chief asked. "Very good for runty pony."

35

"Horse tonic—that's what you sold me," Charley gasped, throwing the bottle from him. "You lied. You said you used to be a little man. . . ."

"Me little when papoose," was the placid answer.

Charley's eyes watered and strong fumes filled his nose and throat. He sat down on the wagon floor and pressed his hands against his burning throat. Fool! You are a dull-witted fool just as Father said, he told himself. When will you learn that you'll always be little—always, always.

For another hour he listened to the rhythmic tramp of the prisoners, then the noise thinned to a shuffling; it was the slow dragging step of a worn-out infantry.

Charley jumped to his feet. "It's Widner's men," was the cry. "Been marching since dawn. We're next. Hoo-ray!"

Thunder cracked overhead.

Orders rang out sharply. "Fall in, men. We're gettin' out of here. On the double—on the double."

There was another crash of thunder and a flash of lightning that illuminated the inside of the sutler's wagon. Then the canvas split open—ripped and torn and hanging from its framework in shreds. Hailstones as big as eggs crashed and rattled all around him.

"March, boys," someone shouted above it all. "March for your lives."

4 Mud and Waiting

A HAILSTONE hit Charley on the side of the head with the force of a rock. He jumped from the wagon and crawled underneath it. On all sides, men were breaking from the line of march to find anything that offered protection. Horses reared and plunged against their harness, officers ceased to shout orders, the whole army was paralyzed. Charley glimpsed Pebbles as she slipped the bridle and galloped out of sight. Other men were crowding under the wagon as the hailstones pounded and rattled above them.

An exhausted soldier almost fell on top of Charley. He was muddy to his hips and his feet were wrapped in sodden rags held firm by manila rope.

"You Widner's man?" Charley asked, staring at his wretchedness. The soldier only groaned. "Let me sleep. Leave me be."

Was this war—waiting, mud, exhaustion?

"Here boy." It was Charley's guard beside him. "Take your popguns. Go home. Act dumb and they'll let a kid like you through anywhere." He shoved the derringers at him.

Charley belted his pistols and shook his head, though his heart beat fearfully. "No thanks but. . . ."

"You little jackass," the guard yelled over the lessening storm. "Can't you see that lots of fellers is goin' to die to-night? But *you* don't have to. Go home!" and a string of profanity poured around Charley's ears.

The hail ceased as suddenly as it had begun, the men came from their shelters in a maze of confusion, his guard disappeared and Charley was alone in the middle of the turbulent army.

Where was Pebbles? He ran down the road and found her standing under the porch roof of a log home. "Why you're really the smartest ding-dong pony in the Shenny-dore Valley," he said, suddenly feeling that she was his only friend.

The Valley Pike boiled with men, reorganizing, pressing the retreat south.

Charley wondered whether to wait for Robert here or begin his own retreat now. Suppose Robert hadn't got the message? This was like holding his hand to a candle flame and couldn't be borne any longer. He mounted Pebbles and rode to the top of a hill where he could look north along the pike. Yes—there were the first units of cavalry to the far right and left of the highway, guarding the flanks of the army. Beyond that, there was smoke and flashes from big guns. Robert was there somewhere, throwing his body and his men's across the path of the enemy army to delay it.

"Go home. Go home." His guard's words seemed to be spoken in his ear again. He turned Pebbles and hastened back the way he'd come. He remembered more: "A kid like you can get through anywhere—just act dumb." He fumbled with the buttons of his shirt so that he could hide the derringers under it, and felt something stiff in the pocket.

The epigram, the providential message to him from Robert E. Lee! Had it been just yesterday morning that he'd worried about a geometry exam and run from school to war? Was he going to run again?

Charley placed his hand over the epigram in his breast pocket. "I'm staying," he swore out loud. "In the name of Lee, and of Jackson too, I'm staying until . . . until the end."

He half expected the declaration to bring a flood of fighting spirit, but it was only his quavering will against the same fear and smallness.

Charley returned to the sutler's wagon. "Got any food to sell?" he asked.

Chief nodded. "Sardines in can. Gingersnaps. Hardtack. For you—little coffee."

Charley paid him and scoured the roadside for equipment thrown aside by Widner's exhausted men. He found a canvas haversack for his food, a better canteen with a tin cup lashed to it, a blanket roll and an India rubber sheet that had been booty from the Union army.

Meanwhile, the sound of battle moved closer; the infantry had gone and horsemen could be seen on top of the hills. Charley mounted Pebbles and waited as the rain began with fresh intensity and the late afternoon darkened unnaturally.

Then a familiar horseman came straight down the pike and Charley knew it was Robert by his horse and by the way he rode.

"Here, Robert. Here I am!" he yelled and galloped Pebbles up the pike. "I was afraid you missed my message."

Charley reined up beside his brother, ready to pound him on the back in an enthusiastic greeting. But his hands went to his sides as he read the expression on Robert's face. It was a keen young face, blurred by a stubble beard and smeared with black gunpowder.

"So it's true. You are here," Robert said in a grating voice. "You'd better go home, Charley. This is no time for a visit."

"But I'm joining up," Charley said. "I'm not going home." He motioned to his equipment. "See—I'm ready."

Robert's tense expression relaxed to a half-grin as he surveyed his younger brother. "You're about the poorest looking little ragamuffin I ever saw. Where did you get such a pony as that?" He put his hand on Charley's shoulder. "Tell you what—there's a family here in Strasburg that'll hide you until the Yanks pass. . . ."

"No," Charley interrupted. "I'm volunteering and if you won't take me, I'll join up with someone else."

A cavalryman rode up beside them and saluted. "Captain, sir, they need you up on Hupp's Hill," he said. "General Stuart's orders."

Robert returned the salute and spoke brusquely to Charley. "Then I'm your officer. Catch up with the last infantry outfit, Louisiana. Stay beside them until I find you. It may be a couple of days before this thing lets up." He turned his horse and spurred northward toward a fresh outbreak of artillery fire.

"We're in. We're in," Charley told Pebbles excitedly. "We gotta march south though." He turned the pony and glanced regretfully over his shoulder. Now that he'd been ordered away from battle, he felt an itching to get into the thick of it; no matter how scared he'd been this time, next time he'd charge bravely on.

Night came quickly from the leaden sky as Charley tagged along beside the Louisiana brigade. He watched them as they built campfires and assembled in small groups to cook rations. Little fires dotted the rolling fields, twinkling like earthstars underneath the tar-black heavens. The messmates nearest him had chosen a spot beside a stone fence and Charley longed to sidle up beside the fire to dry his wet clothes and listen to the soldier-talk. He unsaddled Pebbles, staked her out to graze and walked towards them eagerly.

41

"Hey," he called and noticed how the men jerked around fingering their guns. "Can I sit with you? I joined up just today and I've got some sardines and gingersnaps and things."

There was a silence while the soldiers stared at him. They were a shaggy, bearded lot, except for one too young to shave. "I reckon you'd be right welcome, son," came the drawling invitation. "You ain't big enough to hurt nothing."

Charley joined the circle, emptied his haversack, passed the food among them and received some of their pork and corn pone in exchange. The hearty smell of the boiling coffee on the rain-drenched night warmed the men and one of them exclaimed, "Ain't had coffee in a tarnation long time. We're mighty grateful to you son, ain't we boys?"

There was a mutter of appreciation and Charley was included in the soldier-talk.

"I know exactly what Jackson's a-doin'," a graybeard boasted. "When Ol' Jack got us through Strasburg, he got us outa the trap."

"How's that? I don't feel so almighty safe." The beardless young man took up his musket and hand-rubbed it lovingly.

"Cause of that mountain that begun at Strasburg," the other explained scornfully. "Yanks can't get at us now lessen they come head-on or tail-on, and they're scared to get into it like that."

"Seems like if you're so smart, you oughtn't to be no private." The young man wasn't impressed.

At that moment, the darkness behind them seemed to explode into firing, bugle calls, and pounding, galloping hooves. "Scared, are they?" the young man yelled as they ran for the stone fence.

Charley jumped the wall and lay on the wet grass with them, pouring powder from his flask into the end of his derringer barrel, jamming his hand into his pockets to find the balls and caps. He had one pistol loaded as the horsemen swept into view against the flickering campfire light.

"Let 'em have it," someone yelled and the muskets flashed along the line of the fence.

"No, no. They're Confederate," was the warning shout.

"It's Yanks. Give 'em another!" someone contradicted, and more muskets barked harshly.

The shouts and confusion caused the firing to falter, then spatter sharply again as more and more horsemen piled out of the darkness.

"Fire or we'll be trampled to death," the campfire strategist said into Charley's ear. "Don't you know how to use that popgun?"

Charley took careful aim at a horseman who seemed to command others, and as the man rode into range, he steadied his hand on the stone wall. He would show Louisiana how Virginia could shoot. Then he recognized the figure silhouetted against the campfire, he knew the horse and the way the man rode.

"It's my brother!" Charley screamed. "Don't shoot. They're Rebs—Rebs!" And he knocked his neighbor's gun out of his hands in a spasm of fear for Robert.

By now the cry was general but Charley's flesh crawled with the thought of the near-tragedy.

For hours afterwards, the field was churned into a lake of mud by the cavalry as it checked its flight, regrouped and went back up the pike in a countercharge.

Charley didn't know where to go or what to do until word drifted back through the lines that the front had been stabilized.

"Those Yanks pretended they were our men. Don't fight fair," the men complained. But even this indignant talk died after orders came to be ready to march at dawn. The bivouac settled down as the men rolled up in blankets around the wet, sour-smelling ashes of neglected fires.

Charley spent a wretched night in a damp, half-waking stupor, jumping up at every sound, almost hating the men who slept as motionless as stones beside him.

Reveille, which sounded against the weeping June sky, was welcome to him, and orders to fall in came before there was time to prepare food. The grumbling army stood on its swollen feet and plodded southward again. Charley found Pebbles, mounted and followed after.

But the march this morning was different from yesterday's. There were wounded men from the skirmish of the night before and the ambulance wagons were far to the front. With help from their buddies, the wounded limped along the best they could.

Charley dismounted at the first group and offered Pebbles' services. "She's gentle and you can take turns riding her," he suggested. Then he noticed an abandoned wagon with a smashed wheel on the side of the road. "Say —can't we make a two-wheel cart out of that wreck?"

"Shore we kin," was the ready answer, and the group fell upon the wagon with bare hands and rifle bayonets and stripped it down to two rear wheels and a part of the bed.

"Gimme your belts, boys," someone shouted, "we gotta make a harness fer this blessed pony to pull agin."

"Hope the Yanks don't hurry me none." The belts were thrown in a heap for the harness-maker to use. "It might be embarrassin'."

With many guffaws and jests, the new ambulance cart was set on the macadam and Charley hiked beside Pebbles.

It never ceased to rain all that long day; the men slogged on doggedly despite many stops and unexplained delays.

"It's enough to put a body out of heart," a soldier observed.

"Old Jack will take our sweat but he'll save our hides," came the answer from the ranks.

As Charley put one weary foot in front of the other, he

realized that Jackson's name was magic with his men. They were marching for him—not *for* home or *against* anything—they were simply following Stonewall.

I wonder what he's like. Charley reached up to pat Pebbles. I've heard Father say that Jackson is another Napoleon. I want to see him. I've got to find out how big he is.

5 To Be a Warrior

THE incessant rain filled the rivers to their highest level in twenty years and Charley looked gratefully at the snarling, muddy Shenandoah. The army would cross the bridge, burn it, and while the enemy waited for the water to recede, Jackson would rest his men.

Charley stood beside Pebbles and the ambulance cart, waiting for the Louisiana brigade to file across the bridge. A cheer was raised on the opposite bank, and the soldiers strained to see. "Must be the General a-coming our way," a graybeard said.

"You mean Jackson?" Charley asked. "Comin' here?"

"Don't cheer for nobody else like that! Lawd, lawd, there he comes with part of his staff. Come see, boy, come see." They pushed Charley to the forefront as the crowding men lined the road and shoved the cart along so the wounded could see too. The slouching, sodden army stood on tiptoe for a glimpse of Stonewall. Charley caught his breath, searching for a small, razor-keen Napoleon.

The General and two young officers stepped onto the near bank and the Louisiana cheered. But Charley was dumb and frowned. Jackson was big, but not exceptionally so, he was awkward in the saddle, his horse plain. As the group moved closer, he could see the General's brown beard, the gray uniform spattered with mud like his boots, a cadet cap yanked forward on his head. There was no air of great importance—he was, well, just rusty.

A soldier near Charley yelled, "Say Genril, when we gonna make them Yanks run hawg agin?"

Stonewall turned to acknowledge the question, nodding but not smiling. His gaze swept the group around the ambulance cart and the expression in his blue eyes struck through Charley like saber blades. The intensity that burned there would never dull nor falter; they were the eyes of an Old Testament prophet that Father read about at vespers—like the eyes of Joshua.

Jackson frowned. "What are the wounded doing here?" He spoke to his aide, "Take them up front. Tell Doctor McGuire I sent them personally."

Charley stepped forward, leading Pebbles, and the men shouted approval as the aide whirled his great horse calling, "Make way."

As they trundled across the bridge, Charley heard Stonewall's soft monotone, "Close up, men. Close up. Press on. Press on."

The army had been ordered to pitch camp on the safe side of the river, and as they walked from the tent where the wounded were taken, the aide spoke to Charley in a brotherly manner. In fact, he was much like Robert, handsome, young, educated, a superb horseman. "I'm

Captain Douglas. You've done us a service, son, but do you belong to the army? You don't look a day over twelve or thirteen."

"Yes, sir," Charley answered, saluting as snappily as he knew how. "Sixteen."

Captain Douglas raised an eyebrow. "And have you actually used those weapons of yours in battle?"

"I haven't shot one, but I've aimed it," Charley blurted, and blushed scarlet as he stood at rigid attention.

Captain Douglas burst out laughing. "At ease, boy. You'll soon be a real warrior if you stay with General Jackson." He swung up into the saddle and cantered off through the tent city towards the Shenandoah.

During the next five days it rained in gentle mists, in summer showers and in deluges. The army rested, moved leisurely southward, and at Port Republic sprawled wearily around the southern end of the Massanutten Mountains.

Charley was formally joined to Company F, 6th Virginia Cavalry and soon felt at ease in army life. He answered roll call in his new gray uniform, sweated through mounted drill morning and afternoon, was issued a saber and a new breech-loading carbine. Even Pebbles had a more military bearing as he curried and trimmed her and tied her in the long line of other cavalry horses.

"I'm learning," Charley thought jubilantly. "I'll be a real warrior, like Captain Douglas said, as soon as I've fought with my guns." He jerked his derringer from his

49

belt, loaded, aimed and fired at the knothole in a cedar tree. "Bullseye."

Twice before Taps, Charley went down to headquarters to talk with Captain Douglas, who seemed glad to see him. His brother was continuously far to the outskirts of the army, but Robert and the general's aide were well acquainted.

Tonight, the Kemper home in town was headquarters and couriers and messengers rushed in and out of the brightly lighted house. Kyd Douglas had little time to spend with Charley. The night air was dry now, cool and sharp; soldiers polished their bayonets by the light of their fires, a new hair-trigger tension was building up. Confederate General Ewell was off to the west and occasionally there was the faint rumble of distant guns. There'll be a battle tomorrow here at Port Republic, Charley thought, and the blood pounded in his temples. Finally the door opened and Jackson, nodding good night to his staff, walked over to the corner of the porch. He stood alone, staring into the blackness of the horizon, his head cocked to one side, listening.

Charley watched motionless in the road, half hypnotized by the solitary figure. When Captain Douglas walked over, he muttered, "He's not like Napoleon at all—he's sort of big."

"Ah, but you're wrong," Captain Douglas answered. "Military genius makes them twins. A man isn't measured by his height."

"You suppose I could ever be like that—like General Jackson?" Charley said, speaking his dream out loud into the impersonal darkness.

"It's a bit early to judge," Douglas answered in a merry voice as they walked away. "We haven't seen your courage in battle, you know."

"What's courage?" Charley asked. "Not being afraid?"

"No. Everybody's afraid at times. The coward surrenders to it; the hero pushes fear into the corner of his mind, never forgets his duty, becomes bigger than fear."

"I won't forget," Charley said. He would be that big, at least.

The next morning was a sun-drenched Sabbath as quiet as the Lord's Day at The Grove. Charley sat with several hundred reverent soldiers in front of their chaplain's tent and listened to the sermon. The thought of home caused a lump to swell in his throat and he gazed over the mountains towards Warrenton. The Blue Ridge was the barrier to home, the fortress for the army, the mother that brooded sweetly over the Valley. She stood in smoky blue folds, like a low cloud that faded into the horizons north and south. The camp sat where the little Luray Valley joined the main valley, and up each valley an enemy army waited for the mud and river to allow a new attack. General Jackson was listening to Sunday services in town, while his army rested as cool as a cake of ice between the ice-tong grasp of the enemy. Charley shrugged. If the General had saved them from three armies at Strasburg,

51

he'd have no trouble with two at Port Republic. The soldiers concluded the service by singing a favorite hymn; it was sad, earnest and wistful as the singers thought of the folks at church back home.

> There is a fountain filled with blood
> Drawn from Emmanuel's veins. . . .

Charley drifted away from the group, thinking of Father, his sisters, Unc Ben and the others. The clatter of spirited hooves seemed far away, but when he looked up, a magnificent chestnut horse was almost on him. Charley jumped out of the way, and Sun Bolt flashed down the camp street. The rider was a young, powerful copy of the mountaineer from Front Royal.

"Quinton Hocks," Charley called. "Quint. . . ." He ran down the muddy road past the men who pointed to the horse and turned to stare.

Charley's thoughts went faster than his slipping feet. I'll buy him back. I'll give Quint all my money and even my derringers. I should have told Robert, but it never seemed the right time. Now he'll never have to know. "Quint!" he shouted, but the horseman disappeared toward town, past headquarters and was lost in the supply train that stood south of the Kemper house.

"I can't lose him now," Charley muttered and shinnied up a young chestnut tree, scanning the jumble of wagons with new canvas tops and the sleepy guard. But Sun Bolt had disappeared like a rock dropped into a leaf-littered

pond.   Charley hooked his leg over a limb and stared dis-
gustedly over the long way he'd come.

General Jackson and his staff were coming down the
steps of the Kemper house, and the grooms were going un-
hurriedly after the horses.   There was Captain Douglas,
his horse already saddled and hitched to the fence.   The
conversation seemed to be about the fine weather, but
Charley saw them stop abruptly at the sound of a sudden
whistling.

Boom!   A shell burst right in the middle of town.
Charley clutched the tree to keep from falling out in his
amazement.   Across to the right and in front of the General, a whole mounted company of bluecoats was wading a
little creek.   If it kept coming, the Yanks would be between the general and his army.   Would they realize who
the men in gray were?   Was this the end of the great Stonewall, captured unhorsed on a bright summer morning?

The startled Confederates who guarded the ford broke
and ran toward the supply train; those on duty by the
wagons stared openmouthed and popeyed at what they
saw.   "Yanks!" they yelled.   "How in thunderation?"

Charley saw Captain Douglas offer Jackson his horse, he
saw the grooms frantically scrambling to mount the staff
officers.   The Yanks came on like an angry blue thunder-
head from the right and Jackson refused Douglas' horse
and waited for his own.

"Oh, no—take it.   Take it!" Charley screamed from his
tree.

The men who had fled the ford came piling into the gawking guards of the wagon train. Finally an officer made himself heard and the group began to form into something that resembled a soldier's outfit.

Down in the street, Jackson swung into the saddle at last; one officer was before him, Douglas was third and the others were still unmounted. The three horses broke into a wild gallop, spurred sternly by the fleeing men.

Charley watched the race, clutching the tree and praying harder than he had with the chaplain that morning. Once over the river bridge, the General would be in the midst of his army which must now be alarmed. The enemy clattered up the side street as the three gray figures passed them at close enough range to tell the color of a man's beard and the braid on his shoulder. Pistol shots rang out, but the General's flight didn't falter; he was on the bridge, across it, and out of sight behind the ridge. Kyd Douglas trailed, drawing more fire, and then he too was safe.

The three staff officers who had not escaped were surrounded in the street. A soldier rushed up to the Union commander and pointed excitedly in the direction of Charley's ridge. It was easy to imagine the report, "The supply train is right there. Right within our grasp."

"Oh—they're coming," Charley yelled, and scrambled down from his perch.

"Fall in," he was ordered curtly and the reformed group

from the ford moved against the Yankees. Charley glanced around him. There weren't more than twenty-five Rebs but their captain moved them forward like the whole Stonewall Brigade.

They ran crouching up to the first little ridge that overlooked the street and fell flat on their bellies in the grass and mud. Charley struggled to load his pistols. His hands were slippery with sweat but who would notice if they trembled? What was it that Captain Douglas had told him about courage? He who had tried to give his horse and his chance of freedom to the General.

Somehow he managed to get the powder and ball into the end of his gun, rammed it, and clicked the cap on the nipple underneath the hammer. Then he loaded the other. When the order came, he was ready. The enemy was coming up the street four abreast at a slow but eager trot.

"Fire!" his captain shouted, and Charley aimed his unsteady pistol and pulled the trigger. The muskets beside him spoke with more authority and the strong acid smell of burning powder burst from them in puffs of white smoke.

The enemy troopers broke ranks but their commander rallied them and they came on again.

"Fire!" And Charley emptied his other pistol. This time the volley dropped some, but the bulk pressed the attack. Reloading had to be done without fumbling now.

Boom! Boom! Two cannons from their left unexpectedly lobbed shells into the enemy, who faltered and scattered in the streets.

Down from the ridge where Jackson had disappeared poured a whole brigade of gray infantry, yelling and running like demons over the bridge.

"Advance," Charley's captain yelled. "Fire at will."

He was on his feet, running after the retreating bluecoats. He raced pell-mell down into the street, darting in front of his pounding companions. Gray uniforms were converging from every direction, there was cracking fire and the deep-throated rumble from the big guns on the hill. But the spontaneous victory yell from a thousand throats gushed over every other sound. "Yaaaa–eee–ahhhh!"

Charley felt as if he had wings, he felt bulletproof and immortal, he felt stronger than the strongest, braver than any man. His aim was perfect, he knew, and the derringers almost seemed to load themselves. This was battle, this was glorious, this was breathing scarlet and golden air.

Then he stubbed his toe on the curbstone in front of Kemper's house and sprawled into the mud. But somehow he didn't care as he sat up and wiped the mud from his face. He'd been in battle, fired his pistols no telling how many times, and it had been the most thrilling experience in his life.

6 The Woodpecker

CHARLEY listened to the soldiers' talk as he stood in front of headquarters wiping mud from himself with his shirttail.

"Why, them Yanks like to have caught Stonewall," an incredulous private exclaimed.

"I bet ol' Jack's hoppin' mad now," another soldier said. "Them Yanks start somethin' on Sunday and Deacon Jackson'll pin their ears back."

"Yep—we'd as well commence cookin' rations now. We'll be marchin' at dawn."

The group moved on and Port Republic swarmed with soldiers discussing the day's events in wonderment. Jackson had been spared, the captured staff officers had escaped, Yankee guns and prisoners had been taken; there were congratulations all around.

A cheer came from the bridge as Jackson and Douglas rode back to the scene of their narrow escape. The General seemed to take no notice, but stared at the ground, a slumping, rusty man, a leader who looked like all the things he was except a second Napoleon. Drab as a schoolteacher, stern as a Presbyterian deacon, rough as a mountaineer—until he looked at you with those intense blue eyes. Charley joined the surge of men around the General and the Captain who rode into the pasture next to headquarters and dismounted.

Charley edged forward until he could touch Douglas' sleeve. "I was in the battle," he said. "I shot my pistols, Captain Douglas. I shot them dozens of times."

"Ahh," Captain Douglas turned his attention to him with a quick smile as they hastened across the field in the footsteps of the General. "And were you afraid?"

"Only at first." Charley swaggered a little. "Once I got going, I charged the Yanks without stopping—and towards the last, I wasn't scared at all."

The General was yanking off his gray gauntlet gloves. One of them dropped to the ground as he mounted the stile from the pasture and Charley darted forward and picked it up.

"General Jackson, sir, your glove," he said loudly, proffering it.

The General turned and stared at him as one does whose attention is suddenly brought from deep inner thoughts to the clatter of the outside world. It was a long, piercing gaze that pricked all the boastfulness and Charley saw himself mirrored in those eyes as five feet two with a muddy face.

Jackson took his glove with a nod of thanks. His eyes never ceased to look through Charley; did Stonewall remember the boy leading the ambulance cart at the river?

"Are you a warrior, sir?" he asked in his soft, courteous way.

Charles Randolph stood as tall as he could and returned the General's gaze. *"Yes,* sir," he said, his voice ringing with conviction.

Jackson spoke to Captain Douglas. "I'd like to have this young man attached to my staff as a special courier. Will you see to it, please." And he strode away without another glance, already returned to his secret thoughts.

"Ho!" Charley cried exultantly, a tingling sensation running up his spine and pricking his scalp. "I'm ready, Captain Douglas. Reporting for duty, sir!" He snapped a salute and clicked his heels as he spoke. Wait until Robert heard about this—and Father. "Ho!" he said again, unable to suppress his grin.

Captain Douglas returned the salute. "First, you'll have to be separated from your old outfit. It will require several days, but I'll file for you immediately." He hurried after the General.

The cluster of men moved on as one called, "Bully fer you, son."

"Thanks." Charley hooked his thumbs under his belt beside the worthy derringers. This going to war was downright fun sometimes. The big guns roared in the distance, and Charley knew the artillery and cannons were closer than ever before. But it was the fragrance of the honeysuckle in bloom along the fencerows that impressed him most. Taking big gulps of the scented air, he felt as puffed as a strutting pigeon. Had the valley ever seemed so beautiful? The meadows sparked emerald green, the sky flashed sapphire blue and the two colors clashed and ricocheted in sunbeams. "Ho!" Charley said.

He began to whistle "Dixie." As General Jackson's special courier, he'd need a splendid horse—not humble brown Pebbles, but a handsome beast like Sun Bolt. He ran past the supply wagons and searched until he found the horse tied with three others at the edge of a little woods.

"Sun Bolt!" he cried. Charley rushed forward, ready to throw his arms around the powerful neck. But the horse shied away, trembling with cantankerous high spirits, straining the bridle to the breaking point.

"Temper—whoa now," he crooned, admiring anew the tremendous build of the horse, so delicately made that bone and tendon were clearly defined and the network of blood vessels pulsed visibly under the thin, burnished hide. He was in excellent condition, and there was no sign of the swollen ankle the mountaineer had reported—his legs as clean and hard as chiseled stone. The saddle and bridle were heavy, with many fancy fringes and tooled with swirling designs. How did Quinton Hocks, Jr., come by such a saddle as this one?

"Quint," Charley yelled, running headlong into the woods. The pungent fragrance of frying country ham led him in a few bounds to a semi-clearing where four men jumped up to meet him, hands on holsters.

60

"I—I want to see Quinton Hocks." Charley glanced from one black-bearded face to another until his gaze rested on the burliest of the four. Quint wore a soft slouch hat with the brim curled up on one side, decorated with a gaudy red plume.

The man shrugged. "You're a-lookin' at him," he said.

"Mind if I sit a minute?" Charley asked. "I haven't smelled ham like that since I left home." He looked longingly at the garnet-red meat with its borders of amber fat. The slices lay on halves of old canteens that made excellent frying pans. His mouth filled with saliva as the breeze carried a wreath of smoke to him, heavy with hickory, salt, sugar and condiments. "I'd give a fortune for one like it," he exclaimed. "Do the sutlers sell it now?"

"Naw," Quint replied. "I brung it from home like these here pickles." He reached under a bulging blanket roll and brought out home-canned cucumbers. Charley caught a glimpse of turkey feathers and many more pantry jars. "My maw made 'em. All right, you kin set if you gotta."

"Your mother?" Charley exclaimed. "But your father told me she died years ago." The words grew faint in his throat as all four men turned to scowl at him.

"Let's git rid of this mouse, Quint," one of them said, starting for Charley. "Let's tramp on him—feed him to the cat or somethin'."

"Here kitty, kitty, kitty," the others jeered.

"Shut up. Leave him be," Quint ordered, his mouth

cracking in an awful attempt at a friendly grin. "You must be that Randolph kid that Paw was horse-tradin' with. Ain't that so?"

"Yes—I'm Charley Randolph. That's what I wanted to see you. . . ."

"Rich kid from Warrenton," Quint interrupted, apparently explaining to his buddies. "Lots of land and hosses, lots of money." Quint tore out a splinter from the chopping block, speared a slice of ham and offered it dripping and steaming to Charley. "Set—now jist set and eat a spell."

"Why shore, we was jist a-havin' a little fun with you," the others agreed but still glowered at him.

"Well, I came about Sun Bolt," Charley began, holding the meat uncertainly and feeling like a man watched by a pack of wolves.

"Go on, eat," Quint said. "We got plenty. Come from a neighbor woman that's always treated me like my maw, didn't it boys?" Without waiting for an answer, he flicked out a concealed blade at the end of his pistol and speared a piece of meat for himself. Something about the gesture made Charley shiver. "Well, how you gitten on in this here war?" he asked sociably.

Charley reflected that he could never eat stolen meat, but Quint's explanation set him at ease. "Fine," he said, "I was in the battle this morning and they made me General Jackson's courier. That's why I need Sun Bolt. I'll pay you. . . ."

"You fit in that skirmish today? What with? Not them popguns." The three soldiers pointed at Charley's derringers.

"Yes. With these pistols," he answered, slapping them proudly.

"You musta been in a Yank's knapsack then," one howled gleefully. "Them guns won't carry no further than you kin spit a plug of tobaccy."

"Shut up," Quint said.

But Charley felt his face burning. The men were right. Somehow in the excitement he'd forgotten to take account of the poor range of his small pistols. All the shouting, the charging, the glory—and not one of his bullets had come near the enemy.

"Well, next time," he cried bitterly, "when I get close enough to the enemy, I'll beat him with the butt of my guns."

Even Quint guffawed at this. "Lawd, tell Lincoln to surrender—thar's a woodpecker down here raisin' thunder with his army." The men whooped with laughter, bent double and slapped each other's backs.

Charley stood in the center of the circle, utterly defeated. They were bigger, but more important, his own position was false. He clenched his fists and watched their ugly monkey faces contort with merriment.

When they quieted, Charley shouted at Quint, "I want my horse. Your father cheated me out of him and I want him back."

Quint sobered immediately, ready for business. "What's he worth? How much money you got?"

The others grew silent, their greedy eyes already seeming to pry into Charley's pockets. "How much you want?" he countered, realizing that his wits were his only weapons. "Your father traded even for Pebbles and I don't carry much money with me; I leave it at camp."

"Haw!" exclaimed Quint, seating himself on the chopping block. "It'd take twenty mountain cobs to buy that hoss from me. My ol' man spends his days lookin' fer a lost silver mine—Powell's silver from the Revolution times. Haw! It's still lost. I reckon I know—he ain't never give me nuthin' decent in my life 'til this hoss. I growed up on cornmeal mush and rabbit stew and I don't aim to eat it agin." Quint paused and picked the ham from between his teeth with the blade on his gun. He looked out at Charley from under curling black eyebrows and smiled his hairy best. "But that don't mean I ain't willin' to give you a fair chance at him."

"How's that?" Charley saw two of the men elbow the third, short member of the blackbeards.

The short one answered them defiantly. "You lost too," he said. "Not so much maybe, but you lost too."

"Shut up," Quint ordered them. Then jovially to Charley: "Lookee here, I'll show you jist what they're a-talkin' about." He pulled a small tin snuffbox from his pocket. It was green and decorated with the picture of a deer head. "Come a mite closer so you kin see," he whee-dled as he took off the lid.

Charley glanced hurriedly at the contents of the snuff-box. Then he stared, dumbfounded. "What is it? It looks like a . . . ."

"That's right," Quint agreed. "That's what it is. A louse. The fastest, racin'est, sportin'est louse in this army. Ain't he, boys?" he asked his buddies.

"Same as lightnin'," the short one muttered. The others agreed sourly.

"But how . . . what . . . ?" Charley began.

"Hit's jist a little game we play," Quint said. "You git yourself a louse and we kinda race em, one agin t'other." He reached over to a messkit and took out a tin plate. "Each feller draps his louse right thar," he said, rapping the center of the plate with a thick, blunt finger. "First bug to walk offin' the plate done won that heat. That's all, but it's fine sport."

"I don't guess that's quite all. What happens if *you* win?" Charley asked, pointing to Quint. "Or *I* win?" He jerked his thumb at himself.

"I tole you you'd git a fair chance at that hoss. If'n you kin beat me, you git Sun Bolt." Quint shook his head in imitation sorrow, a gesture that Charley remembered well from his father. "If'n you don't, I gits fifty dollars in cash, right here." He smashed his fist down in the palm of his right hand.

"Oh no—not me." Charley stepped backwards. "Where'd I ever find a louse any faster than yours?"

"Look on any mule or private. Hit's the only way you'll iver git that hoss and if you got any sportin' blood you won't be feared of a lousy game." Quint laughed as Charley retreated. "I'll meet you here at sundown," he bawled.

Charley stepped out into the sunny field again but the day had lost its sparkle.

He left the place with only a longing look at Sun Bolt and went across town to Pebbles. Charley ran up to her and saw how short and brown she was in the long line of tethered cavalry horses. They were a good, harmless, sawed-off pair, he reflected as his fingers wandered through her coarse mane. His eyes followed his fingers intently, and suddenly he had to admit it to himself. He was hoping to find a louse.

7 The Lousy Game

CHARLEY unhitched Pebbles and took her out in the adjoining field to graze. He watched her feed closely like a sheep; compared to Sun Bolt, she looked like a sheep.

Thoughtfully, Charley brought out his money from a belt he wore strapped to his body. He'd only told a half-fib to Quint—there were some loose coins in his haversack in camp.

"Ten—twenty-five—forty-three dollars," he counted. That was a good way from fifty and no new funds coming in until payday. He was helpless without either money or a reliable louse.

Yes, Robert and Father would be proud to know about his new assignment, but wouldn't they snort when they found out about Sun Bolt. And if Robert ran across Quint before Charley had made a clean breast of it—he whistled under his breath. Time had run out on Sun Bolt; either get him back or admit the loss.

"Hey, Mouse," a harsh voice called. "Come over here fer a minute."

Charley jerked around. Quint's short, black-bearded

friend stood in the tent shadows made long by the sinking sun.

"Psst. Come here," Blackie repeated. "I got something to show you."

"What is it?" Charley asked, wanting to turn away, but too curious to leave.

"Come real close. I spec you'll recollect it." Blackie held something in his cupped hands. He began to laugh nervously, his voice surprisingly high for such a heavy man.

Charley put his hand on one derringer. "I'll use it if I have to," he warned and bent over to peer at Blackie's prize.

"Naw—naw. You kin trust me," Blackie said. "What do you see? It's gen-u-ine, boy, gen-u-ine. Had to wait fer ol' Quint to fall asleep to git it."

Charley's eyes grew wide, but he said cautiously, "I see a green snuffbox with a deer head on it." He watched as Blackie quickly hid it in his clothes again, nodding agreement and grinning crookedly. "What's inside?"

"Quint's Lightnin', of course—the fastest louse in the whole Confederate States. And son, they don't make 'em no better than down south." The laugh again.

"So-o. . . ."

"You kin have him free. Jist go back with me and make Quint race ya' like he said he would. You git your hoss, and me and the boys git to see that black bully take some of the medicine he give us." The crooked grin twisted into a bitter, triumphant expression.

"But maybe he won't race when he finds he's lost Lightnin'." Charley began to breathe faster. Was fate playing into his hands again?

"Haw! He might back down fer one of us but not fer any purty little half-pint like you. Not in front of the boys, he ain't." Blackie gave him a shove. "Hitch that goat of yours and let's git started."

Charley whirled around, fists raised, ready to fight. "I don't like being pushed around," he shouted.

But Blackie only looked amused. "Come on. Come on," he muttered.

"Let me see Lightnin'—how do I know you really got him in there?" Charley demanded.

"If you ain't the beatin'est! All right, maybe this'll suit yer highness." Blackie emptied the caps from his cap box into his trouser pocket and took out the green snuffbox. He opened it and showed Charley its occupant, then carefully shook Lightnin' into the cap box. He threw Quint's green tin away and handed Charley the famous louse in his new container. "Now, thar—don't nobody know who you got in thar but you and me. Quint's got no way to know either."

Charley had been raised to judge fast horses, and he tried to look at Lightnin' in the same critical manner. The louse was about a quarter of an inch long, brown, six-legged with claws on the end of each limb—if there were any eyes, he couldn't find them. A shudder ran through him—this was the stupidest, craziest. . . .

"What happens if he loses? I don't have the price."

Blackie opened his mouth and pointed to a hole where two teeth had been broken out. "Quint'll take it out of your hide. But," he added hurriedly, "you don't have to worry none. You got Lightnin'. Now, come on."

With deliberate slowness, Charley tied up Pebbles. This man was obviously a scoundrel and no better than Quint, but he was certainly bent on revenge. The game would be a sort of justice, and besides, there was Sun Bolt.

"All right," he said. "Let's go."

"Hee-hee-hee," Blackie laughed, shaking Charley's hand. "Now you tarry along. I'm gonna git on ahead and set up ol' Quint fer the tarrin'," and he lumbered away.

From both sides of the Massanutten Mountains, there was a continuous roar from big guns punctuated by outbursts of artillery duels. The soldiers of Stonewall's Brigade loitered in front of their tents and watched and listened. Charley walked down the camp street and felt the tension of the silent men; no ribbing, joking—no tall tales, card playing—no cursing or singing. The order had been given—prepare three days' rations—and every half-pint private knew that reveille would sound at earliest dawn and Stonewall's men would march again, not in retreat, but to the attack. He wondered about his own status;

70

would he go with Robert's outfit, with the staff, or—he ran his tongue over his teeth—would he be too beaten up to go anyplace?

As he paced slowly into town, a strident female voice pierced the close quiet of the street. The officer of the day was helpless, muttering, "Yes, ma'am." "No, ma'am." "We'll certainly find the culprits, ma'am."

"Nobody there but me and my granddaughter," the woman said. "And those four black-bearded thieves came right into my very pantry and helped themselves. They made me give them the smokehouse key and even took our gobbler. They weren't Yanks, young man, they were from this very army and I demand to see General Jackson. I demand to know what he's going to do about it and. . . ."

Charley moved on, seeming to feel the piece of stolen ham fester in his stomach. So Quint took from women and children; no dust from his father's poverty would gather on him.

"Little louse Lightnin'," Charley said, tapping the tin box, "avenge the lady, save Sun Bolt, collect for Blackie's broken teeth." He tried to laugh at his own joking, but his stomach churned sickeningly. The shadowy woods were already at hand. Did they ever fight the battles, he wondered, as he heard gruff laughter. Or did they somehow avoid the suffering while clinging to the army like some sucking insect? "Lousy robbers," Charley muttered and walked more quickly towards them.

The semi-clearing was now sunk in evening shadows,

but two fires and candles had been lighted in preparation for the meet. One fire burned close to him and Charley looked inside as he walked past a boiling kettle; he could see fat country sausages bobbing in the churning water and tin plates scattered beside it.

"Gonna have a little feast fer the winner," Quint said, as he motioned Charley over to the group of eight or ten. They were young and rough; all avoided looking at Charley, all eyed Quint with sly smirks.

But Quint couldn't have looked more pleased with life. Instead of scowling and raging about Lightnin's disappearance, he lounged back, well fed, and joked with the befuddled Blackie. Was it an act—was he afraid to show his concern in front of his victims, or didn't he really care?

"Well, Prince Charmin' come like I knowed he would," he cried. "Come set and bring up your louse."

Charley accepted the tin plate someone handed him, knelt down on the ground in the center of the group and placed his louse box in the middle of the plate. "All right," he said. "Let's hear the rules of this game again."

"What's your hurry?" Quint asked, but he took his position across from Charley. The group around them stirred, exchanged quick glances. Blackie laughed nervously.

One of the men volunteered instructions in changing adolescent tones. "Place yer louse in the center of yer plate. First louse that walks clean off the plate wins the course. Three out of five races wins the game. Ain't that right, Quint? That's the way me and you done it that time."

"Right as rain," Quint said, smiling.

"Lightnin' feelin' lucky tonight?" someone asked Quint.

"You'll see," Quint answered, bringing out his louse in an empty pickle jar.

"That there *is* Lightnin' in that jar," a sneering voice asked. "Ain't it, Quint?"

Charley saw Quint's eyes narrow, but he repeated, "You'll see—who's got the watch?"

"Me," Blackie said, crouching beside them. "When I say *Put,* you put your louse down in the center of your plate thar on the ground—fair and square." There was a long pause as he waited for the hand to move to the minute mark.

Taking off the lid of his box, Charley picked up Lightnin' and held him ready to drop into position. The louse waved its six nightmare legs, but Quint's showed no motion.

One of the men hunched Charley. "Lookee thar—he's a-runnin' already."

"Put!" Blackie cried and the two insects hit the tin plates. "Fair and square," Blackie approved.

There was a shout from the men. "Come on, Lightnin'!"

Charley watched his famous speedster as it struck the plate, thrashed its limbs and made its blind, creeping way, toward the rim. Quint's louse sat stupefied, only its two feelers twitching. Lightnin' slowed but finally stumbled off the edge into the dirt and the men shouted, "Hurrah— Bully, bully!"

They expected to see Quint scowl, but the mountaineer's face was a mask. He said nothing, took up his plate and louse and walked over to poke the fire under the boiling sausages. Returning immediately, he got into position for the next course.

"What's the matter, Quint?" someone asked. "Don't you like being beaten?"

Quint spat and hammered his fist into the palm of his left hand. Charley remembered that same gesture had accompanied the demand for fifty dollars if he were winner. "You wanna wear your teeth fer a necklace?" Quint threatened.

"I'm commencin'," Blackie broke in hurriedly. "Ready. . . . Put!"

Charley dropped Lightnin' from an inch above the plate, and the champion began racing immediately. Then he slowed, and slowed, and slowed.

Quint's louse sat dully for an instant, then began to move frantically, all six legs churning and carrying him to the edge of the plate while Lightnin' seemed to lose interest.

"Well, ah'll be!" "If that ain't a caution," the men commented and looked worriedly at the defeated champion, who still poked along aimlessly on his "track."

Charley ran his tongue over his teeth. "That makes us even—one to one," he said.

"Shore does," Quint agreed. "I better check them sausages agin. Thar's a real fine feast a-comin' up fer one of us." He took his plate and insect and went to stir the other fire.

What's he up to, Charley wondered. Even stolen sausage doesn't need all that attention.

But Quint was already in position across from him, hurriedly dropping his shiny plate on the ground in front of him. "Let's git on with it. Didn't I tell you it was a real sportin' game?" Quint smirked at Charley.

"Ready," Blackie said. "Put!"

Lightnin' scratched the tin with his clawed legs for a brief instant, then gradually failed to move at all. "Looks like he's takin' a nap or somethin'," the men commented.

The rival louse hit his plate and scrambled off it like something possessed with a will to win. "That's the beatin'est thing I ever saw," Blackie exclaimed. He glanced quickly at Charley with a sickly grin.

"Waal," Quint said, "if'n I win this next heat, my bug'll have won the game. Ain't that so, boys?"

There was a reluctant murmur of assent.

Quint glowered at Charley from squinted eyes. His fist thudded rhythmically in the palm of his hand and the wordless message sent shivers down Charley's spine. The mountaineer went over again to poke the other fire.

Why—why? Charley thought desperately. What was it about that fire that made Quint's louse win?

But already Quint had returned to position and Blackie laughed shrilly, wincing when he glanced at Charley.

Quint's battered pan dropped into place in front of

him and he held his louse ready. He looked up from under his beetling brows and Charley read the expression of contempt in the crafty eyes.

"Ready," Blackie warned. "Ready. . . ."

Charley jumped to his feet, yelling, "It's the wrong pan! Feel it, men!" He darted forward and grabbed Quint's "track" and tossed it at the group.

"Hot!" "Hot as fire!" "Of all the lowdown tricks," the men screamed. "Cheat!" "You two-legged crawlin' insect!" Someone tackled Quint and the pack seemed ready to follow.

It was enough for Quint. He shook off his attacker and ran, lumbering to the edge of the woods. Turning, his guns drawn, he warned, "Don't foller me. I'll kill ya'."

They heard his footfalls down the path, and then the sound of Sun Bolt's quick, heavy hooves pounding into the distance.

The men turned and looked at each other. "How'd you know? How'd that plate git hot?" Blackie demanded.

"Over there." Charley pointed to the sausage fire. "Look—he's got four or five of them heating. He just took over the cold one and picked up a hot one, only some are shiny and some kind of old and smoked up. That's how I noticed."

"And ol' Lightnin' is jist a dirty louse like any other varmit." Blackie stamped out the champion's life, and rubbed the insect's body into oblivion. "Thar!" he said, and laughed.

A wave of nausea welled up in Charley's throat and the smell of greasy sausage clogged his nose. He hated the men who stood there looking foolish or sullen; they were the weak, pale scum of a great army. He walked to the sausage kettle and kicked it over.

There was a hiss and a cloud of steam as the water doused the coals. He heard Blackie's yell of protest, but Charley kept walking until he reached his own quarters.

Most of the night, he scratched imaginary lice or puffed out his breath to get rid of the smell of stolen meat. His glorious day had ended in a nightmare.

8 The Truth Is Out

I T WAS about four-thirty when reveille sounded and Charley jumped to his feet. The camp had seethed restlessly that night as anxious men fretted to get on with the day's bloody business and be done with it. The news was good, Confederate General Ewell's troops had fought a battle yesterday in the main valley and won. And where would Jackson lead his own Stonewall Brigade this morning? The bugle notes seemed to scream the secret, "There'll be an attack today—an attack today."

Charley's orders were to go with the wagon train which was already moving. He saddled Pebbles and rushed to his post with a pounding heart. Which way would the canvastops roll? Back up the Valley to Strasburg, all the way to the Potomac, even to Washington?

The guard of the supply train was in an uproar. Even before Charley could see it through the early morning mist, he could hear the excited voices of the men. "Ol' Jack's plumb crazy!" he heard. "Maybe our orders is mixed. Shorely we ain't goin' thisaway."

When he had ridden into the midst of the train, Charley watched the leading wagons in bitter disappointment.

South! Away from the enemy. South and east to scale the Blue Ridge.

Charley went slowly to report to the commanding officer who was surrounded by protesting soldiers.

"What in tarnation is this?" the officer yelled at the men. "Treason? Mutiny? I know my orders! You got yours and you better get movin'. The next strawfoot that has anythin' to say about it gits strung up by his thumbs."

The men closed their mouths in tight, angry lines and went about their duty. Officers and mules would never listen to reason.

The train groaned and creaked toward the mountain foothills and Charley was assigned to the rear guard. As he waited anxiously on Pebbles for the last units to move, he tried to hear the sounds from camp. Retreat—was Jackson sick or something?

The sound of strident bugling reached him faintly from camp across the river and he moved back to the very limit of his post. Charley tensed in the saddle; there was the long-roll beat of the snare drum—the signal for the infantry to fall in and march. March, yes, but which way? He was tantalized by the music of the band fading, fading into silence. Ho! So the men were marching in the opposite direction and Jackson was on the offensive after all. He stood in the stirrups and shouted, "Hurrah—go get 'em, boys!" and yelled the news to the guards of the snaking train.

The universal wish came in reply, "Ahh, I'd give a

month's pay to be there." And so would I, Charley thought, I'd even give Sun Bolt if I had him.

"Which pay ain't much, if'n we git it," someone said, but the men grinned and set their horses to the hills. Pay was like the heat; a man couldn't do a thing about it whether it came or not.

All eyes scanned the valley floor from each new height as the wagons wound up the Blue Ridge. At first there was nothing to see but fog that clung to the river; only once a sudden breeze made a rift in the cloud and they saw the columns moving slowly like gray will-o'-the-wisps. Then the valley's mist covered her secret again and the Massanuttens stood sentinel above it, expressionless, brooding over the tens of thousands of lives below. But now they knew where Jackson led his men. Up the little Luray Valley, up to attack the Union General Sigel. No one called out the news this time, but silently added it to the puzzles, the prayers and the fears in his mind. The supply train going one way, the army the other; only Stonewall knew the answer to that.

The foliage of the mountain began to clog out the view of the valley and Charley fell to imagining how it would be with the Stonewall Brigade. They called themselves the foot cavalry because they moved so far so fast, yet there probably weren't a dozen pairs of decent shoes in the whole outfit. He looked down at his own soft cowhide shoes that had been made for him at The Grove. They were badly scuffed but, captured or issued, there would be no shoes small enough for him from the army. The General's courier must certainly have some boots.

Each time the foliage thinned, he gazed anxiously at the panorama below. Puffs of smoke, squat clouds of dust, plumes of dust, the glint of sun on metal—and nothing more but faint rumbling to tell the story of the struggle. The signs of battle looked so small and faded, barely ruffling the serenity of the sprawling valley. Where were Robert, Captain Douglas, Stonewall? Why couldn't Charley Randolph be with them? How could everything be so pale when the whole world should be ablaze with the glory of it? Yet the morning drew out quietly until the wagon train rested in Brown's Gap, astride the top of the Blue Ridge.

An hour later, a courier galloped into the train. "Victory!" he shouted. "Ol' Jack's won agin. He's bringin' the boys up here tonight in case the Yanks come back for more. Heh, heh, you shoulda seen 'em runnin' home to Papa Lincoln."

A jubilant shout rose from the guard. "I knew it," Charley shouted. "No one can beat Stonewall."

"Hurrah! Let's git everythin' fixed nice fer the boys. Even them fellers is liable to be tuckered out."

Charley was assigned to sentry duty while the campsite was prepared. The clatter of hooves brought his attention to the trail; he heard the challenge and then the horseman came on, riding like a cavalier on parade.

A fellow sentry called to Charley. "Say now, that there

is somebody important. You kin tell by lookin' at him.''

Charley squinted in surprise. It was Quinton Hocks—on Sun Bolt. ''Important?'' he exploded. ''To insects maybe.'' But Quint disappeared in the direction of the commanding officer and returned five minutes later to dash down the mountain.

''Hunh! He doesn't fool me,'' Charley muttered.

All night long, exhausted infantry and units of artillery piled into camp on top of the Blue Ridge. Too tired for jubilation, they grinned and lay down on the bare, stony ground to sleep. Next day, both defeated Union armies were withdrawing from the Valley, and soon Jackson moved his men down to the Shenandoah again.

As soon as Charley had discharged his duty, he set out to find Robert. He'd heard that his brother had come through the battle with added honor. Would he be thinking of going home for Sun Bolt to replace his war-weary hunter? Charley urged Pebbles on to the cavalry outpost and entered his brother's tent.

Robert looked up from a copy of a Richmond newspaper and sprang forward happily. ''Ah, Charley, great to see you. Were you in the fighting? The press says that Stonewall is now greater than Napoleon!'' His tall brother picked up Charley and swung him in the air just as he had done when they were both boys at The Grove. ''What's this I hear about you? Douglas sent me word that you're to be the General's courier.''

"That's right," Charley said, and blushed a little from pride and because the General's courier couldn't get his feet on the floor.

The Captain set him down and shook his hand. "Wonderful! But let me look at you. Must say, you don't look the part."

"I know.... If I had my boots...." Charley began.

"Boots?" Robert's brown eyes sparkled. "What the General's aide needs is a haircut, a comb and a cake of soap."

"Aww," Charley said. "I don't have time for that stuff. Not in the army." Would they never stop treating him like a baby?

"Here; sit down and I'll clip off some of your mane," Robert said, laughing. "If Sister and Sadie could see you now, after the way they used to scrub you and straighten the tucks in your shirt. You write to Father—I'm taking a leave to go home tomorrow."

Charley lowered himself humbly onto the campstool. "That's what I wanted to tell you about—Sun Bolt, I mean." And he blurted out the whole story while Robert whacked off his hair close to the scalp.

When the recital was finished, Robert looked at him with less enthusiasm. "So you lost the best horse we ever bred," he said in a grating voice. "You always were too big for your britches." There was a long silence while Charley kept his head bowed repentantly. Good thing it wasn't Father. Father might feel it his duty not to spare the rod, even if Charley were the General himself.

Robert paced the floor. "Well, let's do what we can. I know these mountain people; their land is so poor that sometimes they learn to live by their wits. Money—that's what drives this Quint Junior. Let's offer him a good price, because I've got to have another horse."

"I—I don't think it'll work," Charley said, but followed with quickening step.

A messenger met them and handed Robert a note. "What's this?" He glanced at the paper and read it aloud. "Captain Robert Randolph is to report to headquarters with his brother, Private Charles Randolph, as soon as possible." Robert crumpled the note and rushed for his horse. "Hurry, let's go."

"What's it all about?" Charley cried as he flung himself on Pebbles. "Do you think my new assignment's come through? Do you think they want you to be there when they make me a courier?"

But Robert didn't answer and they hurried into the tent city. A familiar figure paced impatiently in front of the General's headquarters.

"Father!" they cried. Charley tumbled off his pony and ran to meet him.

"Robert—Charles! Are you well?" Father clutched each by the shoulder, his face contorted between joy and tears. "Are you well?" he repeated in a choking voice.

"We are fine, sir," Robert answered. "And Charley's

doing splendidly—he's going to be the General's courier."

Father's expression instantly became grim. "I've come to take Charles home with me."

"Home? Oh, no. No sir. I've got to stay here," Charley cried.

"I think I'm a better judge of your duty, sir," Father said stonily. "The army has Robert. I need you on the farm. The slaves are deserting and taking the horses with them. Saddle Sun Bolt. We'll be riding for Warrenton as soon as I speak to General Jackson."

"You, sir." A sentry came to the tent entrance and motioned to Father. "The General is ready to see you now."

"No!" Charley cried, but Father strode inside the tent. Charley grabbed his brother's arm, pleading for Robert to interfere on his part. "Stop him. He always gets his way, you know he does!"

"We'll see," Robert answered, looking more alarmed than when the trap was about to spring shut on the army at Strasburg. "The General isn't called Stonewall for nothing."

They waited, straining to hear the sounds of conflict between the two men of iron will.

"I won't stay," Charley said, tears close to his eyes. "I'll run away again. I'll fight in foreign wars or. . . ."

"Quiet down," Robert ordered.

Father's irate voice rose audibly from inside. "Charles —under age—without permission—the value of discipline."

There was no answer that they could hear. Then the old Captain's voice was less thunderous. "I tell you sir, that my hay crops are rotting in the field. Look about you; you have thousands of horses that must be fed next winter."

The conversation dropped to a murmur until the tent-flap was thrown open and the two men stepped outside.

Charley stared at his rugged, white-headed father, shaking the hand of the General who was young enough to be another of his sons. "I will say this, sir," Father exclaimed. "If age did not weigh so heavily on me, I'd fight for our country under *your* banner, General."

Stonewall returned the handshake vigorously. "We each have our part to play. No one can say whose is more difficult."

Robert muttered to Charley as they stood in respectful attention, "You're in."

"I know!" Charley whispered, so full of happiness that he paid no attention to the messenger who rode up and delivered a dispatch. The General retired to his tent.

"Ahh, Sun Bolt!" Father said, his eyes lighting at the sight of the best product of his husbandry. "In good hard condition. Excellent. But why does this man have him?"

Charley whirled around and stared up at Quinton Hocks, Jr. He began to explain wildly, stuttering, making no sense. "Well, you see . . . in Front Royal . . . Pebbles is a pony . . . lice. . . ."

Robert broke in, speaking to Quint. "Will you sell your horse? I'll give you five hundred."

Charley gasped and Father flushed hotly. "What's wrong here?" he shouted. "Why do we have to pay a king's ransom for our own horse?"

"Don't shout, Father," Charley pleaded, glancing at Stonewall's tent. "I, well—I had to trade Sun Bolt for a pony to keep out of the way of the Yanks. I tried to get him back in a game of lice. . . ."

"Dice?" Father grabbed Charley's arm and shook it sternly. "Dice? Gambling?"

"No, sir," Robert interrupted hurriedly. "Not dice—lice." He told the story briefly and ended by turning again to Quint. "Let's come to terms now. How much for Sun Bolt?"

Quint sneered as he spoke. "He ain't fer sale. Not fer everythin' you fine gentlemen kin pay me. I'm a big guy to lots of the boys since I got him. Naw, you'll never git a chance at him agin."

"Messenger!" came the quiet command.

They all turned to see Stonewall, who gave Quint a dispatch and dismissed him. He spoke dryly to Father and Robert. "That man's usefulness in the army depends on his horse. I think you should not press him further. Your own sons, Captain Randolph, will serve well under any conditions."

General Jackson turned to Charley. "But you must avoid gambling, young man."

"Oh, no sir," Charley cried. "It wasn't dice, it was. . . ."

Jackson's blue eyes twinkled. "Yes, I heard. . . . Lice," he said.

9 Heaven Is a Long Time

Jackson now turned his forces southward to help drive the Union army from the outskirts of Richmond. Charley waited for his courier assignment as he moved with the supply train. The mountains dwindled away, the sparkling, rolling meadows of the valley changed into flat sandy land, seeping with black water, topped with pine forests and infested with snakes and mosquitoes. The General and his staff were off on secret missions. The heat was intense and the forest became matted with underbrush and vines until it was junglelike.

Robert came to visit Charley at the end of a fortnight, returned from his leave home. "Father is working from dawn to dusk," he said, "even Unc Ben and Sadie are in the fields."

Charley whistled. "That short on hands, hunh? Has Obediah run away?"

"No," Robert shook his head gravely. "Not yet, but he will the next time the Yanks are within hailing distance. You can't blame him—I'd do the same thing in his place."

"Well, I wouldn't," Charley cried indignantly. "You sound like a bluebelly. . . ."

"Wouldn't you?" Robert answered curtly. "Isn't that

what you did? Ran away—to the army. Do you think freedom is any less desirable for him?"

Charley was stunned into silence and scarcely heard the rest of the conversation. New questions were growing in his mind.

Robert went on talking about conditions at home. "And I made inquiries about this Quinton Hocks. Apparently the old man is a good sort—even preaches a bit at times. But rumor says he's gone to hiding slaves from the underground. He's likely to be shot for that."

"Yes," Charley muttered. "He was queer all right."

That night, Charley had a dream. It was about Father in the hayfield, his skin burned dark by the sun, his white hair plastered to his head with sweat, his fingers swollen like sausages from toil. He staggered under a tremendous pitchfork of hay, stumbled and fell fainting to the ground.

The routine of chores beginning another day in the army made Charley forget the dream until hours later as he dawdled beside the tedious advance of the wagons. The thought made him dismount and trudge beside his pony through the blistering heat. Day after day he struggled with his thoughts; he'd have to be a good courier—the best—for that dream of Father not to haunt him. His service to Stonewall had to be more important than Father's need for him. It had to be.

Charley's orders came through toward the last of June; that night he was different from the heavy-hearted youth his messmates had known recently.

"Well, boys, I'm leaving you tomorrow," Charley said as he held his chunk of government-issue beef over the cookfire. "Going up to headquarters."

"Thought you was lookin' mighty purty," a wagoneer said. "Reckoned you'd found yourself a gal."

"Got to be neat and military-looking up there," Charley said. He ran his hand over his fuzzy upper lip. "Anybody got a razor?"

"What fer? Slicin' turnips?" the wagoneer asked.

"Fellers!" One of the guards jumped to his feet. "Seein' as Charley here is a-leavin' us, we ought to give him a present, ain't that right?"

"Shore," they all agreed, sensing a practical joke.

Charley grinned. What was coming now?

"It ain't no gold watch and chain," the guard said sorrowfully.

"It ain't?" someone asked, sounding very surprised, and the men roared with laughter.

"Nope, but it's made by a mighty fine feller—me." The guard groped in his saddlebag and brought out something slender, about a foot long. "Thar—sharpened up the edge of this here broken saber blade till it's same as a razor. Know why?"

The men nudged each other. "Nope. Why?"

"I studied as how I could keep my hoss's mane shaved down close to his hide, but hit didn't work. Too much hair. But Charley, now. . . ."

"Say—les' give ol' Charley a shave," someone shouted.

And Charley went down in a tussle and came up with a red, scraped face. "You look better'n the Ginril hisself," the guard said admiringly. "We're jist gonna give you this here razor as a token of our esteem."

"Hooray. Speech," the men yelled.

Charley mounted an empty ammunition crate, grinning in spite of his stinging face. "I accept with pleasure," he said pompously. "The best skin-scraper there is." He brandished the saber-razor and the men shouted approval.

"I'm sorry to leave you fellows," Charley added, suddenly serious. "But I'm going to be the best courier Jackson ever had. You'll see."

"Well, bully! That's mighty big talk, son," the men declared.

Charley stepped down from the crate. He knew it was big talk and he meant it.

He set off for headquarters the next morning, having plaited Pebbles' mane and tail and curried her until she looked ready for parade. Charley's saddlebag held a comb, a cake of soap, the saber-razor and an extra shirt. With his canteen, powder, shot, and derringers, he hurried to join Jackson. The ditches on either side of the roadbed were seeping with black water, covered with algae, weeds, and wiggling with hidden insect and reptile life. The stagnant water slid off behind walls of jungle foliage and the musk of rotting plants was stifling.

The headquarters flag flew in front of an empty tent; Jackson and his staff were gone and a sullen sentry answered Charley's questions. "I tell you same as all the others what's been here this mawnin'. I don't know where the General is. He didn't tell me. If'n you want him, you'll jist have to look fer him, that's all."

Charley turned away and peevishly slapped mosquitoes that had spotted him and his shining mount with blood. He trotted down the first road to the front and discovered it blocked with infantry moving towards Richmond. Turning back, he hurried to the next side road and found it choked with men standing in the broiling sun, swearing, sweating and beating off the bugs. "Where's Jackson?" Charley yelled. "Anybody seen the staff?"

"Jackson, my aching feet!" they yelled back. "We cain't find a couple of ten thousand Yankees in this pizenous place—same as ants in a hayfield."

Again and again, Charley was forced to retrace his steps as he worked farther to the outskirts of the Confederate concentration. At noontime, he gathered a handful of wild strawberries, drank deeply from his canteen, and took fresh hope in an apparently empty road. Shortly, he heard galloping hooves coming toward him and two cows ran awkwardly into sight. They stopped, two racks of sharp bones covered with hides scarred by ringworm and blowflies; only their eyes were lively with the look of hunted deer. The cows veered to the left, splashed hock-deep into the black water and disappeared into a hidden cattle trail that burrowed through the matted jungle vines.

Charley pulled in Pebbles and listened intently. What had frightened the cows to run them against the general surge of troops to the front? Who was marching towards the Confederate rear? He realized that the sounds of artillery and cannonading, always a rumble in the background, were now audible as separate reports.

Suddenly the end of the road was gorged with dark blue cavalry, pouring down the wilderness trail like a mountain stream through its pass. Charley could never hope to outrun them on his pony. He plunged Pebbles into the black water and felt her sink and flounder in the mud for an instant. "Come on, Pebbles," he cried. "Up the cattle path—up the cattle path or we're done for." But the sucking mud still seemed to hold her. Was it quicksand, he wondered? Did he dare dismount?

When she finally found bottom, Pebbles slogged willingly for the hole in the jungle wall. Charley leaned forward, dropped the reins and threw his arms around the pony's neck. The vines and tree limbs seemed to grab at him and try to scrape him from the saddle, but he clung stubbornly and Pebbles kept stumbling ahead. After the first hundred yards, the vine growth thinned in the sunless depth of the wilderness and Charley sat erect and looked behind him. No one had followed; no one on a full-size horse could get through that tangle.

"Smartest ding-dong pony in the Shennydore Valley," Charley cried as he jumped down into the ankle-deep water. "Old Man Hocks didn't fool me on you, Pebbles."

Quickly he checked the damage; the saddlebag dangled by one strap; he and Pebbles were scratched and wet, but that didn't matter.

Charley looked up the dark escapeway in front of him. It ran straight towards the battle sound. Pebbles reared and a snake slithered under a decayed log at their feet. There was no going back and it was too spooky to stay. He wanted action, didn't he?

Pebbles moved steadily forward on the twisting trail and the underbrush clawed at Charley's clothes and ripped his trouser legs. The thunder of the cannon was as close now as he'd ever heard it and the shriek and explosion of a shell froze him to the saddle. Musket fire rattled on his left and a Minié ball whistled through the woods behind him.

Cold sweat stood in beads on Charley's face, his stomach was heavy and empty, he gasped for breath. He opened his mouth and gulped in the stinking swamp air but couldn't rid himself of the feeling of suffocation. He clutched his derringer with a shaking hand. Why go on? There was no one to know if he turned back. But he made no move, and Pebbles kept on her way.

Puffs of smoke began to eddy through the foliage and the ground level raised to banks of ferns. The forest thinned into a small clearing in front of a log shack, and Charley heard a faint groan from the far side.

"Water," the voice pleaded. "Water. I'm dying."

The tension snapped and Charley was able to move and

think again. He dismounted and cautiously made his way towards the man, cocked derringer in one hand, canteen in the other.

The gray-clad soldier lay on his back, his face blackened with gunpowder and smeared with swamp mud. A chest wound had left its bloody mark on his shirt and stained the ground beneath. "Water," the man whispered.

Charley dropped down on his knees beside the soldier, and held his canteen to the trembling lips. "Here, Johnny," he said huskily. "Here's water. You'll feel better now. I got a pony—take you to the surgeon."

The soldier swallowed twice and choked; a bloody foam flecked his lips. "No," he gasped. "Leave me be. I'm done fer already. Leave me be." He closed his eyes and Charley knelt there, holding his head and wondering if he had died that moment.

"What's your name, soldier?" Charley asked, his voice trembling. "If you can hear me—tell me so I can write your folks."

Charley's question seemed to revive the man. "Yes—my wife—Mary Bly—back home in Front Royal. Tell her the Yanks got me a-goin' forwards, not in the back." The soldier rested a moment. "When the baby comes, tell Mary she should name him Lee Jackson. Say that I'll be waitin' fer her in heaven, but not to hurry none. Heaven is a long time."

After that, the soldier didn't speak any more and Charley continued to hold him while the tears ran down his cheeks and dropped on the blood-soaked ground. Time passed unnoticed and Charley heard none of the sounds of battle.

"Surrender, Reb!" A big Irish voice boomed out behind him. "Faith, what have I got here—a kid and a corpse?"

Charley looked up at the giant Yank with a black handlebar mustache. "Help him," he cried, pointing to Bly. The tears burst out afresh and he felt no shame for them. "Help him if you can—or is he—is he . . . ?"

"Holy Mother, a tender heart in this hell." The man lowered his blue-glinting revolver and examined Bly. "He's dead, lad. There's no help on this earth for him now," he said. "But what are you doin' in this Godforsaken place—you ought to be home at yer faither's knee, by the looks of you."

"I'm a soldier, same as you," Charley answered, placing the dead man's head to rest and standing up to meet the Yank. "I couldn't fool you in this uniform."

The Irishman looked at him for a long moment. "Git along with you—I'm fightin' men, not lads," he thundered. "Me eyesight's bad and it's dark in this bloomin' place. All I see is a lad about the size of me own at home. Begorra, and you better hide yourself and your blasted uniform. There are sharper eyes than mine comin' this way."

Charley stared, not able to believe what he heard. The

great foreign-sounding bluebelly was letting him go. "You mean it?" he asked.

"Get along with you," the Irishman repeated impatiently. "Do you want to get me court-martialed?"

"No sir," Charley cried and darted away to find Pebbles. "Thank you, sir. Thank you."

He pushed every thought and emotion from his mind until he had figured how to hide. Using the razor-saber, Charley hacked a hole in the jungle foliage behind the log shack and hid the pony and himself in the green maw of the swamp.

A snake dropped to the ground from a limb above him. Charley grabbed his derringer and pulled the trigger. Nothing happened but the click of the hammer on the cap. The powder was wet. Pebbles reared, her sharp hooves that were well trained by mountain rattlesnakes flashed wickedly at the swamp moccasin. The reptile uncoiled, hissing hate, and slithered out of sight.

Charley's stomach seemed to turn upside down and he was sick. Yank voices came from the clearing, but he didn't have the strength to care. He felt himself fainting, sinking into the oozing black swamp.

In his mind, Bly's whispered words tolled like church bells: "Heaven is a long time."

10 The Message That Matters

CHARLEY felt someone shake him by the shoulders and the sting of a slap across the side of his face. "You drink," he heard.

"Hunh?" He started up.

"Ssh!" An old woman crouched at his side. "You drink." She pressed a canteen to his lips and he wondered for a moment if he were swallowing boiling water. But it wasn't hot, only fiery strong.

Charley glanced around; he was still beside Pebbles. The woman looked as old as the wilderness, her features a map of the Indian–Negro blood of the swamp natives. "Who . . . where'd you . . . ?"

"Live in shack." She motioned towards the log building in the clearing. "Yanks gone now. You go."

He jumped to his feet and grabbed Pebbles' reins, but his head swirled suddenly and he had to stand there waiting for his mind to clear. "Which—which way?" he muttered.

"Trails lead through swamp from sunrise to sunset—cows go from fresh water to grass." She stood with her head cocked to one side, listening. "Soldiers come. If you hear cry of screech owl, soldiers your kind. Goodbye." She disappeared into the jungle, part of its shadows and unseen movement.

Charley became more alert as he waited for the signal. The jungle was unnaturally quiet as birds and animals hid from Man, his smoke and noise. The gloom had deepened with the coming of evening and the sound of battle was forward and to the left.

"Eee–eeee–eeeee." The signal call quavered through the forest.

Charley seized Pebbles' reins and led her to the clearing. He called down the trail towards the oncoming men. "Don't shoot. Private Randolph—Sixth Virginia."

A dozen Confederate soldiers stared past him to Pebbles. "A hoss! I'd as soon expected to see the King of England."

The group moved on and Charley fell in behind. Somehow they made their way out of the swamp through the increasing darkness, coming suddenly to the road beside an overturned artillery piece with a dead horse still in harness. They pushed on until they blundered into the Confederate camp and Charley found Captain Douglas at headquarters.

The officer glanced at him, smudged with mud, sagging with weariness. "Your quarters are there. Report in the morning," he said.

Charley entered the tent next to the staff's, and fell into an exhausted sleep. The next morning, hunger woke him before reveille and the smell of frying bacon and boiling coffee brought him out at early dawn. A Negro man was bustling around a cookfire in front of headquarters. Charley glanced at the General's tent and the staff's quarters—the bigwigs probably didn't have to get up until late. Suddenly, Captain Douglas' sleep-blurred face appeared at the tent opening. "Charley," he moaned. "Is Jim cooking breakfast already?"

"Jim?" Charley ran over and saluted. "There's a Negro out here. . . ."

"That's Jim—the General's body servant. Sometimes I think Old Jack would rather get us up at the crack of dawn than beat the Yankees." He stretched and smiled. "But Jim makes the best hot biscuits between here and home. Tell him to make some extra this morning. I've never believed a man should fight on an empty stomach."

Charley took the message to Jim, who sent him scurrying to the commissary for more baking powder. After routing out the infuriated officer in charge of supplies, Charley completed his errand as the bugle woke the army. Jim gave him a handful of hot biscuits without comment and sent him back to the wagons for lemons. He had no sooner delivered them than a staff officer ordered him off in frantic haste to summon the blacksmith. One young blood had him search the supply train for black boot polish and instructed him to go to the sutler's for spirits of camphor to repel mosquitoes.

Resentment began to grow in Charley. Hadn't he been designated a special courier—one who carried messages by word of mouth—a station well above those who delivered written notes? Did his superiors think he was an errand boy like the Negro children at home who ran and fetched and shooed the flies away from the table with a peacock fan? He hadn't even seen the General, who was up and out and returned to this tent while Charley searched for spirits of camphor. The infantry was marching, the cavalry dashed through camp, the Virginia swamp churned with history-making events while Charley searched for spirits of camphor. It was too small and stupid to bear. To top it all, when he returned for new orders, Quinton Hocks was there waiting for an assignment.

Charley reined in Pebbles beside Sun Bolt and nodded curtly.

The mountaineer looked down at him. "Thought I heard somethin' a-creeping in underfoot," he said. His laughter added another stab to Charley's injured pride.

A sentry called from the headquarters tent. "You there, on the big horse. Come here."

Quint dismounted and swaggered over to report as General Jackson himself stepped out and handed his courier a message. Charley almost gagged with envy.

"Find Captain Smith—4th Artillery—through the swamp to the first road," Jackson instructed. "Hurry."

"Yes, sir," Quint answered, taking the note. "But I'll have to ride clean around this here swamp, ya know, and it'll take right smart time."

"Ride then!" Jackson snapped.

Quint saluted and galloped away on Sun Bolt as the General watched with narrowed eyes. "Magnificent mount," he commented, but it was obvious that Stonewall was angry.

Charley slid off Pebbles and ran up to Jackson. "I can get through quicker than he can, sir," he said, snapping a salute. "I rode my pony through the middle of the swamp only yesterday."

Old Jack glared at him, his lips straight and stern.

Fear jumped in Charley's mind. Had he been too big for his britches again?

"So you're not afraid of difficulty, eh, Private Randolph? All right, go to it," the General said. "Tell Captain Smith to bring his battery to the front immediately. Hurry."

"Yes, sir!" Charley vaulted into the saddle and raced away. He felt like turning to wave to the General or standing in the stirrups and hollering to every soldier along the way. He knew just how to go, down the road to the upside-down artillery piece with dead horse and beside it was the cattle trail.

He passed a burial patrol gathering the dead, some dressed in gray and some in blue; farther along, the bodies still lay along the side of the road, but Charley looked over them and would not let himself imagine men like Bly or the big Irish Yank. They were part of the desolate landscape, the same as a broken caisson or a shell-shattered pine tree.

As Charley dashed around a bend in the road, he spotted

the overturned artillery piece, and between it and him, Quinton Hocks. Quint had dismounted and was bending over a body of a Union cavalry officer yanking off his boots. A wave of revulsion swept through Charley like nausea. He did not put anything past the man, but this was General Jackson's courier who was robbing the dead.

"Quint, you lowdown black bear," Charley shouted. "Leave the dead man alone! Jackson told you to hurry."

Quint only glared at him and continued what he was doing. "Don't bother me none, Pretty Face. Ain't no sense in burying a fine pair of boots like these here. I kin wear 'em." One boot slipped off in his hand and he bent to pull the other.

Charley shuddered and yelled. "Leave him alone! You're no better than a buzzard!" He jumped from the saddle, seized Quint's arm and jerked him away from his prey. In an instant, the mountaineer's horny fist hit him under the chin and sent him sprawling on the road.

"Remember this," Quint said. "I kin break you in two any time I take a notion. It ain't none of your business what I do."

"That's what you think. I made it my business." Charley jumped up, watching Quint's gun hand and rubbing his jaw. "I told the General I can get to Captain Smith before you. I can ride through the swamp in half the time you take to go around."

"Tryin' to git me in bad with the Ginril, eh?" Quint looked narrowly at Charley. "Yep, I reckon you kin creep through that stinkin' jungle like a rat in his burrow." He slapped Sun Bolt's neck and ran his hand over the great shoulder. "Could be a Yank sharpshooter would put a bullet in that there runt hoss of your'n. You wouldn't be goin' no place very fast then."

The sweat trickled down Charley's face and into his eyes. Here they stood, Jackson's couriers, delaying their orders to squabble between themselves. He knew this was a threat from Quint, but he couldn't let him feel challenged to carry it out. Charley turned to stare at a dead horse that lay stiff legged in the ditch. Suddenly, he whistled in appreciation. "Say, I didn't know the Yanks were that rich," he said. "Looks like this saddle is silver-studded." He began to walk toward it, glancing at Quint from the corner of his eye.

Greedily, Quint's gaze followed, his whole attention fixed on the muddy Union saddle.

Now, Charley thought. It's now or he'll know it's a trick.

He yanked out his derringer and fired into the ground at Sun Bolt's feet. The big horse reared and plunged, jerking Quint off balance, reenacting the scene in front of the Front Royal store.

Charley jumped astride Pebbles and galloped up the road toward the cattle trail; if Sun Bolt were as cantankerous as he used to be, there'd be time to make his escape.

"Ho—whoa, you devil hoss!" Quint yelled at his mount. "I'll learn you."

Sun Bolt answered with an enraged whinny.

As he plunged the pony into the jungle, Charley got a good look at the two. Dust rose from the road as Sun Bolt reared and struck with his front feet. Quint shouted abuse and jerked the bridle reins cruelly.

Charley ducked through the pulling vines and pushed his pony as fast as he could, the thought of Jackson's steely blue eyes spurring him on.

So he was going to be the best courier the General ever had, was he? Charley knew he deserved the guardhouse or worse for neglect of duty—ten minutes for a stupid quarrel while tens of thousands of men marched dutifully to battle counting on artillery to cover their charge. And where was Captain Smith's battery? Charley turned the knife in his conscience. Why, Captain Smith had never received word of his orders and men fell dead in the field because his guns were not there.

"I've got to hurry," he thought desperately. "If I carry a million more messages, I'll never stop a second until they're delivered—even if it's only spirits of camphor."

He came to the fern-filled clearing and wondered if the old woman were peeking through the chinks in the log shack, if the burial party had found Bly's body, if they ever would. But he didn't hesitate or take his eyes from the path in front.

Suddenly the empty forest was sliced through by a road swarming with marching men. Charley called for information about Captain Smith's battery and had soon delivered General Jackson's message to him. As he finished, he flushed and added weakly, "I was delayed and the General meant me to come as fast as possible."

Captain Smith nodded. "I understand. We'll lather the leather getting there. The boys been hankering to get a crack at the bluebellies."

After that, Charley made his way to headquarters again. The General and the staff were gone, Quint had not returned and he spent an hour waiting for orders. The sound of artillery fire at the front grew louder until the earth seemed to tremble as new batteries arrived and Yankee guns gave back better than they got. Captain Smith had had time to come up and the duel was reaching a peak. After this would come the attack. If only he could hear the blood-rousing Rebel yell as the gray line surged against the Yanks!

He saw Captain Douglas riding through camp towards the front and Charley galloped after him. "Please, sir— can't I go with you? You might need a courier for something."

Captain Douglas' face was haggard and his horse wet with sweat. "Yes," he said wearily. "I can use you. Have you ever been under musket fire before?"

Charley thought of the stray bullets that had whined around him in the swamp. "Oh yes, sir . . . not a real battle, but I've been around lots of shooting."

"Not in a real battle." Captain Douglas repeated the

words grimly and sighed. "Well, the General's aide-de-camp needs an assistant so there's no help for it. Come on."

"Then I'm assistant aide-de-camp," Charley said delightedly and grinned at his friend. "Just for this afternoon, I mean."

The officer nodded and his eyes twinkled briefly. They rode forward side by side, and the Captain began to talk to Charley as if to himself. The noise of battle cut out many of his words but the gist was audible . . . "artillery duel all day, . . . we're losing . . . an hour or so until dark . . . an attack up Malvern Hill is still possible but the cost, the price. . . ."

The bullets began to drop around them on the road, and Charley forgot everything except steeling himself **to** act like Douglas. He gathered the reins in his left hand and let his right rest casually on his knee. A small branch along the roadside fell into the ditch, clipped off by a bullet. The hair on Charley's neck bristled, but he wouldn't allow a muscle to twitch. They turned off the road into a woods that bordered flat farm land, and passed through the infantry, crouching in the shelter of the stripped pines. All eyes strained forward and Charley knew that up ahead was Malvern Hill. Case shot and shell fell through the umbrella of treetops; smoke from Federal batteries drifted down upon the gray lines and Charley was frozen in his nonchalant pose.

"Wait here," Captain Douglas ordered. "Keep your eyes open so you can tell me what you see. I'll return shortly." He disappeared into the forest.

Suddenly, there was a yell from the right and it was caught up and repeated along the Confederate line. The woods itself seemed to surge forward and Charley, hypnotized, followed in the infantry towards the wheatfield. A country home, spotted around with outbuildings much like The Grove, sat on the other side of the farmed fields and waving grass mounted a steadily rising hill beyond. Cheering, Confederate troops advanced across the open ground; they rushed straight up the center of the hill or clambered more slowly up its steeper sides. Floundering through the woods, new infantry came up and followed the attack.

The Union batteries on the crest poured down fire that seemed to sweep every foot of open ground. Charley saw half of one regiment fall like hay before the sickle, another drop down singly as apples from a storm-battered tree. A third reached level ground near the crest only to hesitate and slump to the earth.

Smoke blotted and blurred the dim twilight and a tornado of sound deafened Charley's ears and mind. The Confederate lines began to slip back down the hill, some cowered against it for protection, his countrymen lay on the field like gray leaves strewn upside down by hurricane winds.

"Back at them. You can't give up," Charley yelled. It

108

was just as Douglas had said—the price . . . the cost. . . . "Charge 'em again."

It had seemed like a week, but it must not have been long, because the Captain was jerking him by the shoulder and shouting.

Without hearing what was said, Charley followed numbly towards the road. General Jackson was there, sitting on his horse, staring at the panorama. He received messages from frantic couriers and only nodded in response; shortly he sent Douglas on a mission and the others also. Finally, Charley realized that he was the one closest to the General on the entire battlefield.

As Jackson moved about, Charley trailed, ready to act as courier. The battle ceased to seem real—only the effort to appear unafraid was his true concern. Every time the General's blazing blue eyes rested on him, Charley pulled himself up tall in the saddle and clamped his jaw.

Night came on. Other officers and couriers came and went, but Jackson seemed to want Charley riding quietly beside him. Opposing forces were all mixed up on the hill, and the lines could only be distinguished by the flashing of muskets. The glare of big guns spread a bloody flickering light through the woods, and the world was made of weird shadows and roaring sound.

Rain set in and hours later the battle quieted and the moaning of the wounded began to be heard. The staff reassembled beside Stonewall as they returned towards headquarters.

"We have been whipped," someone said. "It was murder for our side."

"General," an officer asked, "do you think they'll counterattack in the morning? It would be disastrous, sir."

Jackson rode with his chin thrust out and up, his cap pulled down over his eyes. His answer came in angry defiance, "No sir, I will not hear to it. They will be gone in the morning."

Charley fell asleep in his tent, drugged by weariness and the weight of desperate sights and sounds. One man's judgment alone seemed to stand between them and catastrophe tomorrow; Stonewall could not fail now.

Next morning, the Yanks had withdrawn from Malvern Hill.

11 A Whole Bit

CHARLEY had one sheet of linen paper that he had borrowed from Captain Douglas. With a quill pen from the same source and the sutler's faded ink, he was trying to write a letter to Front Royal. He wrote carefully, using the bottom of Pebbles' water bucket as a desk.

Dear Mrs. Bly,
    I take my pen in hand to tell you that. . . .

He stopped and chewed the end of the quill as the scene in the wilderness came sharply to memory. There was so much to tell the widow that his stiff pen would not write.

    . . . I regret that I was with your husband when he died.

No! That wasn't it. Charley crumpled the paper and threw it away. As soon as possible he'd ask leave to call on Mrs. Bly and visit Father too.

He turned to his messmates, who were preparing breakfast. This was the last of their coffee, so he sipped slowly and let it trickle down his throat.

From the next cookfire, he heard Quinton Hocks' voice and saw him slap his boots with the flat of his hand. Quint had formed his own group of messmates, and as Charley stared, he observed Blackie and heard the high laughter. Probably Hocks had invented a story about the boots, since even Blackie's kind would not stomach robbing the dead.

Charley sauntered over and stared curiously at green watermelons hollowed out from end cuts. Good, he thought, fruit like that would give the whole bunch a bellyache. "Say, Quint, did you ever deliver your message to Captain Smith?" he asked.

"Shore," Quint growled at him. "You think I want to be a target for a firin' squad?" He kicked the cook fire with his fine Union boot. "Reckon this purty gent will stick up his nose at our new business, eh boys?"

Blackie and the other smiled and nudged each other just as they had before the lice game. "You bet I would." Charley turned his back on them and stalked away. He wasn't dumb enough to mix in their affairs again.

He rinsed his tin plate in the stream and strolled to headquarters. It was two days after the Battle of Malvern Hill and the Confederate army was slack and bleary-eyed from losses.

General Jackson sat in front of his tent on a campstool, his booted feet held rigidly with toes pointed straight ahead. He received reports and gave terse orders. There must be a tightening of discipline; it was time to jerk up the Army of Northern Virginia by the scruff of its neck. Completing this business, Jackson nodded to Charley and the two mounted and trotted hastily down a wilderness road. Where the woods broke into a meadow, the General said, "Wait here," and went forward into the center of the field. He paused and looked around expectantly, glancing at his watch.

What's this, Charley thought. Who could Stonewall be waiting to meet? He touched the paper in his pocket and drew out the epigram, "A foe may give lessons in fighting, but life teaches learning." Yes—his heart thumped wildly—yes, here he came.

A gray-bearded general on a gray horse rode quietly into the clearing. Jackson was quick to dismount and the two men greeted each other courteously, then paced up and down the field in deep discussion. The one plodded like a farmer, the other moved with ease and grace.

Yes, Charley thought, it *is* General Lee. I'll show him his school paper if he comes this way. I'll tell him I'm his cousin. I'll say that Father is fine thank you, and. . . .

But the rendezvous was already concluded and each man returned his own way. General Jackson looked at the note in Charley's hand. "A message for me?" he asked.

"Oh, no sir," Charley said, but handed it to him. "You can see it, sir. It belongs to General Lee, who's my cousin though I've never met him. I found it in our schoolhouse at home."

"Ah yes," Jackson said, glancing down and returning the epigram. "My confidence in your cousin is so great that I would follow him blindfolded."

"But you're the one who's greater than Napoleon," Charley answered. "The Richmond papers say so."

"They are mistaken," Jackson said. "It is not I but God who gives us these victories."

Charley returned thoughtfully towards camp. Hadn't he seen the eyes of Joshua in this man? Hadn't he waited outside the tent with others while the General finished his devotions? Didn't he need this strength himself? From now on, he wasn't going to forget to say his own devotions.

The General turned in his saddle. "Do you understand the meaning of your epigram, Private Randolph?"

"The words are simple," Charley answered, amazed at such a question. "I'm sure I do, sir."

"I'm just as certain you don't," Jackson said abruptly, but his expression was kind.

They rode through every corner of the camp, inspecting the ground, watching the drilling men. The General brought out a lemon which he sucked while going his rounds, finally throwing it to the ground, limp and flat.

Six weeks passed like this as the army moved northward on the Warrenton side of the Blue Ridge. The valley soldiers threw off the swamp lethargy and sang their mountain songs. They drank coffee made from scorched ground sweet-potato skins and ate fresh sweet corn from the fields. Charley was close enough home to reach it in a half-day's ride—or night's ride, since the Yanks still occupied Fauquier County. He asked for leave and received a forty-eight-hour pass beginning at taps.

Charley waited impatiently by the sentry an hour before time. It was a hot August night and the sentry grumbled incessantly about his thirst. Finally, he said, "Randolph, stand duty fer me fer ten minutes, will ya? I'm gonna git me a sip of watermelon."

Obligingly, Charley stood guard until the sentry returned and then set off himself with a thirst for a cool slice of watermelon, following the man's directions.

"Right here's your watermelon," a voice cried from in front of a tent. "One bit fer the bes' ye ever tasted." The man laughed peculiarly.

A line of soldiers stood waiting to enter the melon tent, and Charley pulled out his paper money to select a bill for 12½¢—a whole bit should buy a big piece of melon. The customers who entered apparently departed from the rear, and from inside the tent, Charley heard, "One . . . two," and then a cough and a splutter. The line moved closer and he heard again, "One . . . two." Cough. Splutter.

Just as he gave the barker his bill, Blackie's high-pitched laughter and Quint's familiar roar came from inside. Charley snatched at his money. "Oh no, I'm not going in there. Give me back my bit."

"Like squash, you ain't," the man replied and shoved him inside. The tent was half lighted and several dozen watermelons were stacked on the dirt floor. But it was behind the fruit that a soldier was kneeling, his mouth pressed against two straws that dipped into a hollowed-out melon rind. Blackie squatted beside him, the side of his hand inches from the man's Adam's apple. The soldier swallowed once and his Adam's apple bobbed. "One . . . ," counted Blackie. Then another swallow. "Two!" Blackie hit the man's throat with the side of his hand cutting off his ration and the customer left the tent spluttering and coughing. "Next," Blackie said. "Waal, I declare, look who's here, Quint."

Quint struggled up from the floor behind the biggest pile of melons. He stared tipsily at Charley, "If it ain't the Ginril's purty lil' pet."

Charley fingered the butt of his derringer. "I paid for watermelon. Give me a piece of this one." He thumped an uncut melon with the toe of his shoe.

"Git your two swallers and shet up," Quint ordered. "Thar's watermelon juice in thar along with some huckleberry mash, raisins and tater peelin's—nice and fermented."

"No." Charley deliberately loaded his pistol and watched as Quint clumsily drew his. The man was half drunk from sampling his own moonshine. "If there's any shooting in here, the duty officer will be mighty surprised at what he finds. I'm not taking your brew—only a slice of melon like I paid for."

Quint poked his head through the tent flap and yelled at his customers. "Git! Shop's closed. We're gonna have a picnic in here and you fellers don't know how to act at no picnic." Then he turned to Blackie. "You git too. You ain't no gentleman."

As Blackie hastened away, Quint flicked out the concealed blade in his pistol and slashed at the melon, as if,

Charley thought, it were the belly of the General's pet. He drove the knife in to the hilt and raked it down lengthwise, stabbing until the melon split in two, red inside and the juice flowing. He looked up at Charley with bloodshot eyes, his breath heavy with the smell of his one-bit product. "Think you're smarter than me! I got you skun seven ways."

"Just give me the melon," Charley said, but cold sweat popped out on the palms of his hands.

"Shore. I owe it to you to give you the best." Slowly, he began to carve out the heart. "Paw made me promise to give you some money each payday on that hoss—that was afore he'd tell me where Sun Bolt was hidden in the mountain. I promised but I ain't paid you and I never will. Paw, he's crazy dumb—always a-preachin' and a a-pratin'—a regular slave lover. I hate Blacks." Quint looked up expecting to see quick agreement.

Charley stepped back, wrestling with his thoughts. Hate Sadie, Unc Ben, Obediah? No! He didn't even hate the Yanks—only this other southern white man. "I don't," Charley said furiously. "I don't hate anyone except a man who acts like a drunken black bear."

Quint kicked the watermelon across the tent in reply. His tongue seemed to wag beyond his ability to keep it quiet. "You wanna know if'n I went clear around to Captain Smith? Heh, heh, oh I went after I finished a-pickin' up stuff from fellers-who-won't-need-it-no-more. I got money now—I got Sun Bolt—and I ain't takin' no chances

117

on gittin' that hoss shot up either." Quint laughed and lunged at Charley, his fists swinging wildly.

Charley dived through the wobbling knees, upsetting the unsteady bulk, and ran for the rear of the tent.

"Come back here," Quint yelled, "or when I ketch you, I'll loosen your teeth of a certain . . ."

"All right," Charley cried, sprinting around to the front of the tent. He stuck his head through the flap and grinned toothily. "Here I am—come get me." And he darted away, laughing. Even a powerful man with a foggy brain was not half as big as he.

When taps sounded, Charley mounted and galloped into the night, happy to be going home and glad to forget Quint. The moon was full and the road lay clear between meadows made misty by dew and silvery light. A huge oak stood out lonely against the sky, casting its own black pool on the ground. A rail fence jutted crazily to the right and left and laid its irregular shadow on the road. Charley passed the last Confederate outpost and rode quietly into no man's land.

It would not be a good night to slip through the Yank lines with the sky so aglow. He turned into a pine woods and the clop of Pebbles' small hooves was muffled by the bed of needles. They moved on to more and more familiar ground until the way led over a high ridge that marked the far boundary of his father's own land.

"Ho! We've come through the Yank lines without knowing it," Charley told Pebbles, and urged the pony out of the woods towards the open hayfield, feeling safe because he was home.

"Halt," came the sleepy challenge. The sentry was only ten feet away in the broad black shadow that marked the end of the woodland.

Charley was so surprised that he only dropped down and hugged Pebbles' neck and let her trot slowly in the other direction.

"Forget it," another voice said. "It's only another one of the Old Captain's heifers he's hiding from us. They don't understand Yankee language no more'n he does."

Yanks on Father's land! Captain Randolph of The Grove, who killed every bobcat that strayed to his farm, who marked his boundary by the mound of dirt that would last hundreds of years. And the enemy had invaded Father's domain as if it were the wilderness waste. Impossible, yet he should have known.

Charley tied Pebbles in a clump of pines and worked his way toward the house. He scrambled on his stomach through the damp grass of open ground and ran in the shadows, crouching and darting from one safe spot to another. He passed Cabin Hill, sneaked around the stable and up the garden path to the back door of The Grove.

12 Loyal Tom-Tom

CHARLEY raised his hand to knock on the door but stopped himself before the first tap. How could he be sure that Father was inside? Perhaps the enemy occupied the house.

He crept to the side of the garden and yowled like a bobcat. If the Yanks were there, they'd not care but Captain Randolph would come immediately with gun and hounds. Charley screeched again.

There was no answering uproar from the hounds in the kennel yard and only one bass voice barked from inside the house. It was old Tom-Tom, the hound who led the pack on the fox chase, his baying known to every farmer and sportsman in the county. Then Father flung open the door and strode into the moonlight. "Come out into the open, whoever you are," he shouted. "I've heard enough bobcats in my time to recognize a real one."

Tom-Tom gave a yelp of joy and frisked over to Charley, who ran forward from the shadows.

"Charles!" Father said softly, embracing him and hurrying him into the house. "Charles, you're not safe here. The Yanks use my home whenever it pleases them." There was righteous indignation in the old man's voice.

He lighted a candle and closed the blinds to hide its flickering light.

"I'll only be here a short while," Charley said, and went on to explain about Mrs. Mary Bly. As he talked, he mentally checked the familiar items in the sitting room which was dominated by an enormous stone fireplace.

"That's ridiculous." Father almost snorted at the proposed ride to Front Royal. "Forty miles in and out of enemy territory when a letter would suffice."

"But I couldn't write it—I tried weeks ago and our army may not be this close to Front Royal again." Charley stared at the floor, ashamed. "Besides, I owe it to her since I didn't write at first."

"Yes, you do," Father agreed. "So you must pay through the seat of your pants for your lazy brain. As soon as the war is over, you're to return to school."

Oh no, Charley thought. Someday he'd tell Father how he wanted to stay with General Jackson and after this war was won, they'd go any place in the world that needed a general and his courier.

Instead, he told his experiences; Father must realize how important this job was that kept him from The Grove. Captain Smith became a Major or even a Colonel to whom he'd carried a Very Important Message. Excitedly, he crouched in various corners of the room to show the relative position of the forces at Malvern Hill. "That was the day Captain Douglas made me assistant aide-de-camp and. . . ."

Father scraped back his chair and hurried to the window. He cracked open the blind and the sleepy light of dawn was background for the close sound of horses' hooves on the pebbly drive. "Yanks," he whispered. "Quick son, the fireplace."

Charley knew what he meant; only last fall Father had boosted him up to inspect the inside of the chimneys. He had been furious, not because of the dirty job, but because he was the only boy on the farm small enough to work all the way up through the narrowing channel and out onto the roof.

The fireplace was large enough for a man to stand erect and Father raised Charley on his shoulders until he had a foothold on a rim of brick inside the chimney. "Don't move about," Father said, "they'll hear you."

There was a harsh banging at the door and Tom-Tom answered with a snarling rush. Charley scarcely breathed as he heard Father walk ponderously to the door, slapping himself as he brushed the soot from his shirt.

"Open up—in the name of the Army!" The voice seemed familiar but all Yankees sounded alike.

Father opened the door with the firm announcement, "You've no right here. . . ."

"Captain Randolph," the voice interrupted—it was one of last night's sentries—"we know you're hiding livestock from us. . . ."

"You're exactly right." It was Father who interrupted this time. "I consider it my duty to hide everything from you!" And the door slammed shut amid an uproar of threats and the snarling of the dog.

There was a lull and Charley hoped the Federals had ridden off; it was going to be hard to get through the enemy to Front Royal without a disguise. He looked at his hands that were black with soot and realized what he could do. A ragged black boy would ride on a dusty pony through the Warrenton countryside—so unconcernedly and on such a dull mount that no member of an invading army would look at him twice. Busily Charley smeared his face, arms and legs and tore his shirt to look more ragged—the shoes were fine, the Confederate insignia was easily ripped off and the pistols belted beneath his shirt.

Crash! It was glass shattering from the window in the room below.

"We're coming in to get you—you blue-nosed Rebel," the sentry yelled.

Charley understood now that the Yanks must have requisitioned all the firearms in the house and Father would be helpless. He jumped down, drawing his derringers and peered around the corner of the fireplace.

Father stood against the wall beside the window with a heavy chair poised in the air, ready to bring it down on the first head that came through the broken window. The two sentries looked very young and bluffed by the situation. Suddenly one of them whirled around. "Great Caesar's ghost! It's the Major."

Charley glimpsed the Federal officer dismounting and

the two privates snapping to attention. Frantically he up-ended a log, used it as a sloping ladder, and kicked it away. Clawing and clinging, he regained his foothold on the rim.

Then he heard the officer demand of Father, "What's that blood-thirsty hound of yours doing in the fireplace like that? You've tried everything else—have you stuffed some of your cows up the chimney?"

Charley glanced down the black channel, hardly breathing. There was Tom-Tom directly below, looking up and wagging his tail.

"He is expressing appreciation for his hearth," Father answered. "You gentlemen have left us nothing—not even two hounds, but we are still blessed through your generosity with our own hearth, sir." His tone was acid with sarcasm. Then he shouted, "You will ultimately pay for your outrages."

But the officer was not overawed. "Captain Randolph, I can't stop to discuss this with you. I've quite a journey ahead of me today. However, I must warn you that your continued rebelliousness will bring retribution. Good day, sir."

There was a long silence until Father's voice came in a hollow whisper from below. "They've stationed a guard at the front door, but he won't observe you if you leave by the chimney. You can climb from the roof into the trees. I'll go out and berate the guard. He'll not be able to hear himself think. Goodbye, Charles, Goodb...."

Father's voice choked, he could not finish the word, but moved to the front to bellow, "You interloper—you bandit. Get off my property."

Charley edged out of the black shaft into the blinding sunlight and dropped to the roof on the far side of the chimney. He rested a moment, hearing Father's tirade below and then grabbed an overhanging locust limb, and began to work his way from the house.

He saw that Cabin Hill was deserted, that the stable and barn were empty, that there was only Unc Ben pottering pathetically in the weedy garden.

For the first time, something in Charley cried out in the angry voice of his father. The enemy had no right to do this to them. No, there was nothing he nor anyone else could do at The Grove now. General Jackson must save them; victory was the only thing that mattered any more.

He reached Pebbles and rubbed her with red dust as Tom-Tom came running to him. But Charley ordered the hound home, and riding like a plowboy, slumped and loose on his plodding mount, went quietly down the farm road. He stopped and traded a farmer his cap for a tattered straw hat that hung down over his ears. The man understood when he saw Charley's straight brown hair and the deal was readily made.

Heart thumping, Charley rode through the back streets of Warrenton. Yanks were everywhere, busy and important as the townspeople kept out of sight as much as possible. Only Ben Healy, who had come from someplace in

Delaware a few years ago, stood on the street talking with the bluecoats. No one noticed the colored boy until Tom-Tom's bugle voice announced that he had not gone home but was following Charley. Mr. Healy had hunted behind Tom-Tom many times as Father's guest, and now he stopped talking and stared after them.

He knows, Charley thought, not daring to speak to send the dog home.

It was already too late to turn around when he saw the roadblock at the far side of Warrenton.

"Who are you?" the sentry demanded. "Where you going?"

Charley cocked his head so that the hat brim blocked his face from the Yank. "Isaac—jist Isaac," he said in the mournful, thick accent of the slave boy. "Gwine to see Miss Sally."

"Miss Sally who? Why?" the guard asked as he fended off the growling Tom-Tom with his rifle butt.

"Jist Miss Sally up the road a piece," Charley said, edging Pebbles away. "She gwine be eighty-fo' years old this summer—sent for me to clumb up her tree and pick peaches for p'serves. Miss Sally make the bes' p'serves in this heah county."

"Git going then," the guard snapped as he sidestepped Tom-Tom's threatened rush. "Call off your hound and clear out of here."

"Yas suh." Charley whistled and plodded down the road.

Around the bend and out of sight of the soldiers, Charley slipped off Pebbles and thumped Tom-Tom's sides in hearty congratulation. "You scare off more Yanks than the whole Confederate army," Charley chortled. "But you got to go home. Go on now—go home!"

Tom-Tom's delighted air wilted and he turned dejectedly, moving a few steps and glancing back at his young master. Finally he slunk into the weeds by the roadside and Charley mounted and rode hard towards Front Royal. Up into the cool mountains and down once more into the Shenandoah Valley that was as hot and steaming as a blacksmith's shop this August afternoon. Thunder muttered from the west like the disgruntled voice of the sweltering valley.

Charley was nearly famished for water and dead tired, and every inch of Pebbles was wet with sweat. He turned off the road at the first shaded creek and drank until his stomach felt heavy. He found Pebbles pasture grass and, snuggling against the cool bank, fell asleep.

Two things woke him; a crack of thunder from the approaching storm and the wet, rough lick of Tom-Tom's tongue across his cheek.

"Oh!" Charley jumped up. How much time had passed? He looked down into the hound's hopeful brown eyes, grinned and hugged him. "You stubborn rascal—you ought to be home but I'm glad you're not."

The road had seemed deserted for half a day but now the Yanks were in evidence again. Charley's procession trailed through the village of Linden as the wind rose and lightning flashed on the horizon. They were safe, he thought, if the hound would not draw attention to them.

A group of blue-coated officers stood on the corner of the street watching the storm advance up the mountain.

"Tom-Tom," Charley muttered under his breath. "Steady now. Heel. Behave yourself." His voice reached a pitch as the hackles on the dog's back began to rise and he made a stiff-legged advance on the nearest officer. "Tom-Tom, heel!" Charley cried and the group turned to stare at him.

Charley hardly dared to move in the saddle as he plodded down the road. The dog obeyed grudgingly but a crisp Yankee voice said, "I'd know that hound anywhere. He darn near bit my leg off at Randolph's this morning." It was the voice of the officer who had sent him scurrying up the chimney.

"Hey—hey, you boy," the Major shouted and started after them.

"What's got into you, Major?" another Yank voice called. "He's just a kid." But the footsteps behind never faltered.

Help me, Charley mentally repeated, dear God help me. If I run now the whole bunch will be on me.

"Keep that dog away or I'll shoot him," the Major ordered as he seized Pebbles' reins. "Are you one of Randolph's people from Warrenton?" He looked searchingly into Charley's face and his eyes narrowed.

"Yas suh," Charley muttered. "I'se Isaac—ol Captin sent me to hep Miss Sally. . . ."

Then everything in Linden seemed to explode there in the road. Tom-Tom made his rush for the Yank. Charley threw himself off Pebbles in a vain effort to grab the dog. The wind came in a mighty rush and the straw hat sailed off his straight brown hair. Lightning struck a chimney behind them and the rain came down in torrents. The Major's pistol blazed and the hound's leap was cut short as he fell dead at their feet. The officer made a grab for Charley, yelling, "A spy—I knew it."

There was a chance. The storm was a gully-washer and it was impossible to see or hear twenty feet away. Charley jumped on Pebbles and zigzagged down the road in a wild gallop. Bullets zinged past them as the Yank followed on foot; then there was nothing but the gray curtain of the storm.

He was riding now for his life. A spy would be shot. The alarm would be spread and they would begin to hunt for him. The Yankee major's suspicions could be confirmed by Mr. Healy back home—and he'd probably do it.

Pebbles' hooves splashed in the water as it coursed across the road, red with mud. Charley thought of the gallant Tom-Tom, who never stopped fighting as long as he lived and whose blood also ran red in the water. The raindrops hit hard and drove into his face so that he couldn't see and he tasted the salt of his tears in his mouth.

13 *The Spy*

EVERYTHING depended on luck now. He could only ride into Front Royal not knowing whether the Yanks were there and ask the first person for Mrs. Bly. Charley grabbed his shirttail and scrubbed his blackened face. Probably the best plan was to ask Mrs. Bly how to escape to the Confederate lines again.

Pebbles' way led downhill to Front Royal and Charley pressed on to the crossroads store. A group of men lounged on the porch watching the storm begin to clear. "Where's Mrs. Mary Bly live?" he called.

"Mary Bly? Oh, you mean Arch Bly's widder," the storekeeper answered. "First log house down by Happy Crick. That-a-way," he said, jerking his thumb. "Where you from, son. . . ."

But Charley didn't stop to answer curious questions. The rain was lessening and the Yanks might be riding after him from Linden at this moment. As soon as the little log house came into sight, he began to yell, "Mrs. Bly—Mrs. Bly!" and vaulted from the saddle, running towards the front door.

He rushed into the only room, which was spacious and clean with a loft above. A woman stood by the wood range heating her flatirons and a boy of eight held some small sticks as he tended the fire. They stared at him, looking half indignant and half frightened.

Charley stopped and tried to remember his manners. "Uh, excuse me, ma'am. The Yanks will be coming after me—and I wanted to see you privately a minute. I've a message from your husband before . . . before. . . ."

The woman's hand went to her forehead as if she might faint, but she steadied herself by leaning against the ironing board. "Yes. Set down, young man. I. . . ." She reached down into a big basket of laundry and handed her son a red checkered tablecoth. "Soldier, did you come from Linden way?"

Charley nodded.

"Git then, Archie," she said. "Jist the same signal we always use."

The boy took the cloth and obediently went out into the drizzle of rain.

"Set down and relax a little. I'll watch fer the signal and you kin rest easy," Mrs. Bly continued. She could have been twenty-five or forty, sturdy, marked by sorrow and hard work. "I declare, I niver saw a man look any hongrier." She opened the oven and brought out a green apple pie and set it in front of Charley.

"Oh, no thank you—I couldn't eat a whole pie," Charley said, his mouth squishing with water and his eyes devouring the golden crust. Obviously this household had no food to spare.

"You're welcome to all of it," Mrs. Bly said. She walked to the window and stared off toward the hill that rimmed the town on the Linden road. "I'll watch. Now, tell me about . . . about my husband."

Charley relived that day in the wilderness. He told Mrs. Bly everything, just as it had happened.

"Yes," she said intermittently. "Yes, that was so like Arch." Tears glistened on her cheeks.

"And he said to name the baby Lee Jackson," Charley concluded, glancing around for a cradle.

Mrs. Bly's clouded expression broke into a proud smile as she turned to a laundry basket and picked up an infant for Charley to see. "There he is," she said, "Lee Jackson Bly. Finest name I ever heard." She snuggled the baby close in her arms and stared out the window while Charley devoured the pie, all of it. Maybe the Yanks weren't coming after all. Maybe they couldn't be bothered about a spy who was "just a kid." But no, the Major would bring them.

"Well, I got to go, Mrs. Bly," he said, pushing back his chair. "I'll pay you for the pie. Things must be hard for a widow and. . . ."

"Deed not," Mrs. Bly said stoutly. "I take in washin' —we still got our cow, the hens and a hawg or two. But there it is—the signal. Quick!"

"Where?" Charley jumped to the window and searched the horizon. The tablecloth hung from the branch of a tree on the hill overlooking the Linden road.

"Archie just seen the Yanks come around the fer bend in the road," Mrs. Bly said. "When they come 'round the near bend, he'll take down the cloth before they kin git at him. Everybody in town knows the meanin'."

Charley rushed out the front door to Pebbles, his voice cracking with excitement. "How shall I go? How about to Strasburg and down the Valley?"

"Mercy, not that. The Yanks is all over Strasburg agin." Mrs. Bly shook her head. "I was wonderin' how you aimed to get out of Front Royal. There ain't but one way I know."

Charley gathered the reins and sat ready to gallop according to her instructions.

"Halfway down the Strasburg road," she said, speaking rapidly, "turn to your left on a mountain road. There's an old man there three or four miles in what will hide you and. . . ."

"Quinton Hocks?" Charley exclaimed. "Not Quinton Hocks?"

"That's him," she said, surprised. "The bushwhackers say he oughter be shot fer smugglin' slaves, but I say he oughter git a medal fer hepin' our own boys the way he does."

"I know the road," Charley said, watching as the tablecloth disappeared from the tree. "Goodbye. Good luck."

"God bless you," Mrs. Bly called, and stood in the road waving as long as he could see her.

"You're heading for home," Charley told Pebbles as he urged her to top speed.

Glancing towards the Linden road, he saw horsemen top the ridge. "Here they come," he said and turned from the road to let the pony pick her way through the mountain forest, where the Yanks could not spy them with binoculars.

Pebbles' instinct led them unerringly to the clearing behind Quint's cabin. "Hello!" Charley shouted. "Anybody home?"

"Waal, dad-shame!" Old Quint strode out of the forest with his musket slung easily in the crook of his arm. He seemed very surprised but Charley figured that the mountaineer had been watching their approach. "Waal, shoot me fer a horned hoot owl. If it ain't little Randolph still a-ridin' the smartest ding-dong pony in the Shennydore Valley."

Charley greeted Quint gladly; the old man was just as he'd remembered, tall, sinewy with skin like leather and eyes that flashed humorously as he spoke. "Can you hide me from the Yanks," Charley asked, "and help me get back to Jackson tomorrow?"

"Shore I kin. We better shake a leg," Quint said. "I wondered what was a-eatin' them Yanks ridin' out of Front Royal like hounds trailin' a rabbit. And you was the rabbit all the time." He laughed and led the way quickly.

They climbed up rock slides, over ridges, down a ravine and at last Quint indicated an abandoned mineshaft behind a clump of cedars. "Thar," he said, "I'll bring you some grub when I kin. Set low," and hurried away.

Charley led Pebbles into the mineshaft with him and stared around excitedly. Hadn't Quinton Junior said his father was prospecting for a lost silver mine? Could this be it? He dropped to his hands and knees and gathered some small rocks and took them to the light, but they were tan, gray and reddish, just like any other handful of pebbles. Ten feet back, an earth slide had closed the shaft, and the ground was dotted with black splotches from frequent cookfires. Something glinted in the light and Charley picked up a link of metal chain, the raw edges still bright where the chisel had cut through. He shivered. This must be a part of a slave chain. He had never seen a man in chains except a convict. Most of the slaveowners would no more fetter a difficult Negro than they would a trouble-making son, but he'd heard tales about it. Charley threw the link from him with all his strength; he wasn't fighting to keep chains on men, but only to have The Grove back again like it used to be. He shook his head and refused to think about it any more. If Lee and Jackson would lead, he would follow.

Twilight came while whippoorwills called and bats flitted in and out of the shaft. The moon rose and the night filled with the buzz of tree frogs, crickets and cicadas. Cool air seeped out from the woodland and Charley waited anxiously for the old man to bring news and food. He looked down at his thin arms and legs, ran his hands over his sides and the ribs felt like a washboard. He smiled at the thought of the time the Indian sutler had sold him horse tonic to make him grow; he was smaller than ever now, not only short but skinny.

An hour later, Old Quint came silently from the woods and handed Charley a wooden bowl of lukewarm gruel. "Here's your grub. T'ain't fancy but hit'll hold body and soul together," he said. It was rabbit meat and corn meal stewed in water and Charley choked it down.

"Did that boy of mine pay you somethin' on yer horse?" Quint asked, squatting on his heels.

"No," Charley answered. "I guess it doesn't matter except for Robert's sake. Pebbles is more my size and a heck of a lot smarter."

"I done wrong by you, though I meant it fer good fer the boy," the old man said. "But my son's no good— a-lyin', a-cheatin', and a-robbin' whatever he can. When I find my silver, I'll pay you myself."

"Is this it—the silver mine?" Charley asked, pointing to the shaft.

"Naw, ol' iron mine, only good fer hidin' people in trouble." He turned to Charley and his voice was curiously restrained and flat. "The neighbors say they're gonna shoot me for hepin' men in chains—the Yanks say they'll shoot me fer hepin' men in gray. But if'n they'll hold their fire a few more weeks, I'll have my silver. I know now where it is—hit's got to be."

Charley reached out and grasped the old man's arm. "I hope you get your silver—you've earned it."

After that, Hocks led the way on horseback southward along the crest of the Massanutten Mountain, finding trails that were invisible to Charley, avoiding ravines and taking advantage of gaps to scan the black valley between them and the Blue Ridge. Before dawn, they came down from the hills, cantered across the sleeping farm lands, crossed the river and plunged into the mountains again.

The old man turned in his saddle. "Waal, here's where I leave you. Jackson's acrost thar." He indicated the Blue Ridge still to be scaled. "Take keer. I wish my boy was like you, little or no. . . . Don't let no tadpoles give you a thrashin'." And he trotted down into the morning mist that clung to the river.

Charley silently saluted the disappearing figure; old Quint didn't give a hang what folks thought of him. Big or little, Charley Randolph knew he shouldn't care about his size, but he did—though not as much as a couple months ago.

14 The Greatest Feast in History

CHARLEY joined Jackson above Culpeper and traveled over the same way towards The Grove, this time on duty with the plodding army. Since he knew the territory so well he usually rode quietly beside the General. The staff stopped ordering him off on errands for themselves and the soldiers began to point to him and smile. "That there's the General's mascot."

Charley was proud to have his name associated with Jackson's, proud too that the men liked him. They were a strange lot, who fought for their general almost beyond human endurance, yet no one could train them to be proper soldiers. They ambled past him now in ragged shirts and trousers of every description, many without shoes, hats and caps decorated with feathers or no hats at all. Some pitched away their blanket roll and haversack, preferring to go without when the going was rough and hot. They walked like coon hounds, loose-jointed, all bone and stringy sinew, their bellies pinched and their cheeks hollow. Johnny Reb was hungry but he was independent as long as he breathed.

The General breakfasted every morning now on cornmeal mush, and Charley usually finished his own meager ration and stood waiting outside Stonewall's tent.

This morning, Quinton Junior waited on duty beside him, as fat and spit-and-polish as a Yankee. Charley said gruffly, "I saw your father the day before yesterday."

"S'at so?" Quint shrugged. "Dumb as ever, I reckon."

"He is not dumb," Charley retorted. "He's almost found the silver mine—he told me so himself."

Quint guffawed. "Heared that everyday since I was hatched."

"Well, he got Sun Bolt for you. That wasn't so dumb," Charley said.

"He niver got me nuthin'." Quint's face was suddenly livid. "Everythin' I have, I got myself. I couldn't a kept Sun Bolt without the lice game. . . ."

The argument went on more and more loudly until the General strode out of the tent, his whole manner one of irritation.

"Attention!" he snapped. "I will not tolerate this, gentlemen." And he sent Quint galloping in one direction with messages and Charley in the other. Afterward, when Charley rejoined him, the General's lips were tight and Charley knew he and Quint were on probation.

"There were plenty of Yanks close to here the other day, sir," he said. "We're bound to run into them soon."

"Of course," Jackson agreed and that afternoon the guns opened up in an artillery duel at Warrenton Springs. The staff assembled beside the General and the group

139

rode forward together, led by Charley through a short cut to the scene of action. The site of battle was a great horseshoe of white buildings, a famous resort beside the mineral springs.

The Confederate battery was wheeled up between the hotels and the disputed bridge beyond. The air was filled with shrieking as ragged-edged shells were forced from the barrels of the cannons. The Federal artillery sent back shrapnel that burst overhead and spread small balls like birdshot over the area; solid iron cannon balls sometimes crashed into the Rebel-held buildings. The General rode back and forth on his horse directing the fire of the guns, though repeatedly warned of the unnecessary risk he was taking. But Charley didn't worry about the General. He knew that Stonewall was invulnerable and had begun to feel the same way about himself. Many were killed, more escaped and why shouldn't he be a lucky one?

Towards evening, Quinton Hocks rode up and Charley could tell that Quint was scared; his color had blanched, perspiration beaded his forehead, and he frequently gasped for breath. The magnificent Sun Bolt rolled his eyes and the flesh quivered under his satin hide.

The Yankee fire became more accurate and Jackson was compelled to seek the shelter of a ridge with the others. Charley saw him look at the newcomer, his penetrating glance reading the signs of fear; his eyebrows raised as he turned away. A shell screeched overhead, flashed and exploded, scattering shot directly behind them.

Another shell whistled close and Quint seemed to think it was meant for him. Before it could explode, he had not only released his tight rein on Sun Bolt, but spurred him in the sides as well.

"Uh–oh," Charley yelled. "He's taking his fine horse away from here!" And there went the black bear of a man on the fire-and-victory horse, running like a scared circus act—spurs flashing, elbows flapping, hat tumbling from his head.

"General, look!" Charley rushed up to Jackson, holding his sides and screaming with laughter. "Look," was all he could say as he pointed to the disappearing figure.

Horse and rider topped the hill with spurs still jabbing the runaway to greater speed—only Quint's headgear was left on the ground to prove he had met with a living Yank. The whole group was convulsed with mirth and even Jackson threw back his head in a wide-mouthed laugh that was drowned by artillery explosions.

"Don't you think we'd better move on, sir?" Captain Douglas called.

Jackson nodded and added, "Prefer charges against that man."

The group trotted away, but Charley lingered behind, chuckling to Pebbles. "Did you see it? Did you see old Quint sock the spurs into him?" He laughed so hard that tears came into his eyes as Yankee shells began to bombard the hotels in earnest. He stood on a little knoll close by, remembering the times he'd visited these buildings with Father.

Suddenly there was a new sound added to the explosions of shells—an undercurrent of sustained crackling. Charley stared as fire leaped out of the upstairs windows of a wing of the hotel; there was a direct hit on the pavilion, which burst into flames and illumined the gathering darkness. This had been the famous vacationing spot of three presidents and yet it was disappearing like a tinderbox. A side of a building fell in with an eruption of sparks flying high against the black sky; the roof caved in and the faggots set other buildings on fire. Charley turned away—the fountain, the deer park, the bowling greens, the waltzing ladies would never be here again. Part of the old way of life was burning up before his eyes. How much more, he wondered, would go like this?

The bridge was cleared and the army moved northward towards Manassas Junction. No supply wagons now, but three days' ration in the haversacks, which the men ate immediately since it was safer in their bellies. Twenty-five miles yesterday on apples and roastin' ears requisitioned from the farmers' fields; twenty-three miles today and always the order from Jackson, "Close up, men. Press on, press on."

Charley heard the soldier-talk as the army plodded on quietly. "Folks hereabout say the Yanks got mountains of food at Manassas. If'n I tucker out, boys, you all tote me on and lay me out in the middle of the 'lasses jugs and coffee beans."

There was a hearty mutter of agreement and an exchange of solemn promises. No one must miss the capture of General Pope's commissary.

The cavalry reported that the way was clear, the Yanks had left everything in their hurried retreat. And Charley, looking down on the plain of Manassas, saw more food than he had ever dreamed was in heaven. One hundred railroad cars packed with delicacies, warehouses bulging with staple goods, and the sutler's stores so rare that many a Rebel had never seen nor heard of them.

At first, there was an effort to distribute systematically, and Old Stonewall ordered all discoverable whiskey dumped into the ditches. Then the order came for every soldier to help himself to four days' ration and Charley gorged himself on the first food he found in the railroad cars—canned sardines, horehound drops and licorice candy. He stuffed his mouth with the contents of a whole sardine tin and drank the oily liquid; while he ripped open another can, he crammed his cheeks with candy, sucking and chewing. Its smoothness and sweetness felt like heavenly manna on his tongue so accustomed to salt pork and parched corn. After his craving had been dulled, he began to look more discriminatingly for the shoes and coffee that he needed.

There were many strange sights as he moved among the jubilant troops. A private looked helplessly at the spilling sacks of coffee, his pockets bulging with candles and soap, his haversack full of flour, cakes and oranges, his canteen sweet with molasses and sugar in his cup. With a yelp of joy the private solved his problem—he whipped off his cap and filled it with the precious beans.

Another soldier strode by with a beaming face—he had a full load of nothing but French mustard.

Charley scooped up all the coffee he could carry in his haversack and pockets, and saw one soldier use his shoes as containers. He passed a sutler's tent where troops were handing out black seegars, filmy linen handkerchiefs, and soft underclothing fitted over grimy, lice-bitten legs. Soldiers passed him draped in shoes, five or six pairs tied together by the strings and worn like beads. But though he looked for an hour, Charley couldn't find a single pair small enough for himself.

Off somewhere to the north the Yanks counterattacked and were driven away and the frolic went on undisturbed. The messes had begun to congregate, showing their prizes. "Lawd, there's everythin' here from a dose of quinine to harness hames," someone yelled, and his buddies whooped until they were hoarse.

Charley took his accustomed place beside the General who began to inspect his celebrating men. His expression was more and more dismayed until he saw a mess throw away a side of bacon in favor of a dozen tins of pickled oysters.

"What's the meaning of this?" Jackson thundered.

144

"You, of all people, should not be guilty of wasting food."

The soldiers jumped to attention as one of them called out, "Jubilee, Ginril, jubilee! This here's the greatest feast in history! Ain't that so, boys?" And the whole group cheered as Jackson turned his horse away, his blue eyes half stormy, half amused.

Charley had six cups of coffee for lunch, hot, black, fragrant and strong. Then the swapping and bargaining commenced; a pound of coffee was worth a dozen tins of canned fruit with a bar of soap thrown in. Charley began to see that his booty would fill his saddlebag with tins and still provide a cup of coffee every blessed evening.

Someone pulled at Charley's sleeve. "Massa Chollie, suh. Please suh."

He whirled around at the soft, familiar voice of Unc Ben. The old Negro clasped him in his arms with tears in his eyes. "They burned hit down. The Yanks burned hit."

"The hotels?" Charley asked. Could Unc Ben have come twenty miles to tell him that?

"No suh." Unc Ben drew him away from the crowd. "Let me tell you 'bout it over heah to ourselves."

"It's Father then," Charley almost whispered.

"They tuk him off to prison up no'th some'res," Unc Ben said, his woolly white head shaking as if palsied.

Charley's mind swirled and he felt as if the blood were draining from his body. He listened numbly as the old slave relived that day.

" 'Twas that ol' Yankee Major that was always a-strut-tin' 'round the farm like he owned it. Three or fo' days ago, he come to the Old Captin. 'Gimme yo keys,' he say.

"Ol' Captin, he just look at him, and start a-bellerin' that he ain't gonna do it.

" 'If'n you don't, we'll burn this place down to the ground,' the Major say, lookin' mean out of his eyes. 'I got reason to believe you was a-hidin' a spy in dis here house. Our army is withdrawin' and we's a-takin' what food they is with us. Hand over the keys to yo smoke-house!'

"But Ol' Captin begun a-tauntin' him. 'You ain't with-drawin'—no sich thing. You jist runnin' from Jackson—jist runnin'.'

"The Major, he grab his pistol and pint it at yo father. 'Gimme them keys,' he say and he mean it too.

"He got 'em all right—he got 'em." Unc Ben rubbed his hands together at the memory. "Ol' Captin take a holt of his key chain with all them sharp little keys and give it to him—right acrost the mouth. Yas suh, he slap them right in the Yankee's face and the blood start a-squirtin' from his lips.

"The Major, he call the guard and they marches Ol' Captin away. Then they sets the curtains in the parlor on fire—and when the roof fall in, the sparks gets to the stables, and after dat, the barn . . . and. . . ." Unc Ben's voice was too choked to continue.

"I know," Charley said. "The house and everything

else burned one after the other, like the hotels." And in his mind's eye, he saw The Grove in an orange, red and yellow holocaust, with little blue flames dancing on the doorstep. He saw his father glancing back at it as they took him away from Fauquier County to a Yankee prison. Anger grew in him until his mouth had the taste of bitterness. They sat there brooding until the orders came for the Army of Northern Virginia to stand on its feet again and start marching.

"Send me some boots," Charley cried to Unc Ben. "Here, take all this coffee and sell it back home—and take what money I have." He shook his fist in the direction of the enemy. "I'm going to need them bad. I've only begun to fight!"

15 Glory! Glory!

CHARLEY rededicated himself to his job. Through a series of bitter fights that the press called the Battle of Second Manassas, he carried more and more important messages until the General began to look for him first when there was real work for a courier. War might be his business in life, here today, and later wherever battles could be fought for a livelihood.

As the army plodded towards Frederick, Maryland, the villagers lined the streets to see the great Stonewall Jackson. Some of them tossed flowers to the boys in gray but occasionally children defiantly waved the Union flag. Here, brothers in blue and gray often faced each other.

"Oh, look," a young girl squealed. "There's Stonewall himself."

"Yep, and I bet that boy beside him is his son," someone said. "They sure do look alike—so serious and all."

"Bet he is, at that," another agreed. "See—they even set their horses the same way."

Jackson turned in his saddle and looked at Charley, who flushed self-consciously. But the General gave him an amused wink and the two rode solemnly past the pointing villagers as rumor preceded the army on its line of march.

Straggling in enemy territory was particularly hazardous and Charley carried messages to the brigade commanders. General Jackson wanted the ranks closed up and the strictest discipline was to be used to enforce the order.

The ranking officers nodded agreement, but the junior officers who must perform the duty shrugged a little helplessly. Johnny Reb's independent nature hadn't changed since crossing Mason and Dixon's line and straggling had always harassed his superiors. Riding through the troops, Charley kept his eyes open for Quint whenever he saw a guard with gray-clad culprits. He approached men carrying fence rails on their shoulders, or doing double time on a barrelhead, and those wearing placards stating their shame as they were drummed through camp, but Quint was nowhere with these petty offenders.

Charley asked Captain Douglas about it one evening around the campfire.

"Hocks had a general court-martial this morning," the Captain said. "And you better get over there first thing. He's not going to need your dad's horse any more."

"A general court-martial?" Charley was shocked. Such action was for traitors and criminals. . . . "Ohh," he said. "What did they find out?"

"Got him on five counts. A supposed friend of his named Blackie something-or-other turned informer." Captain Douglas sounded disgusted as he counted off Quint's offenses on the fingers of his hand. "Cowardice, neglect of duty, selling bootleg whiskey, robbing the dead, stealing from civilians—and heaven knows what else. The court wasn't inclined to clemency."

"Good!" Charley said. "But he'll be all right? I mean, they won't shoot him or anything?"

Captain Douglas gestured as if to dismiss the subject. "Oh, he'll be safe enough, and for a very long time."

So—he could have Sun Bolt, Charley thought, dazzled by the idea once again. But the next morning, he reached down and slapped Pebbles' humble brown neck. "You know, I don't want that crazy brute," he told her. "But Robert'll probably need a new horse since he got that promotion."

After much searching, Charley found the guard taking their convicts to the rear of the army. The prisoners wore metal collars around one ankle and a chain secured to a heavy iron ball which they were obliged to carry. There was a black bear of a man shuffling along in the line and Charley rode up and questioned the officer in charge. "What's his sentence?" he asked, pointing to Quint.

"Hard labor—ball and chain for the duration of the war," the man said. "And, ssssst. . . ." He made the sound of something searing and motioned to his cheek.

"Can I talk to him?" Charley asked.

"Shore—jist keep movin'," the guard said.

Charley dismounted and walked beside Quint. It didn't seem right to ride above him now. "Where's Sun Bolt?"

"I sold him," Quint muttered without taking his gaze off the ground.

"But you couldn't. . . ."

"I said, I sold him," Quint repeated dully. "I jist kep a-goin' after that hoss run away. I tuk him clear to whar I could git gold fer him." Quint turned on Charley and a big letter *C* had been branded on his cheek, the mark of a coward. "Hit'll be death to you to see that hoss agin," Quint cried. "If'n Sun Bolt's rider comes after you, he'll stomp you under foot like a squashed toad. Death—death to see your own hoss." He laughed wildly and quickly lapsed into dull silence again.

Without answering, Charley watched the line of wretched figures shuffle out of sight. Quint's half-crazy threat stuck in his mind; it would be death for him to see Sun Bolt again.

The week following was one of easy glory, as Jackson wheeled around and recaptured Harper's Ferry with eleven thousand Union troops and thirteen thousand small arms without firing a shot. Then at one in the morning, Stonewall's men began a march that even the General termed severe. They were rushing to Sharpsburg, Maryland, to join General Lee and others against overwhelming forces of the enemy under McClellan. There was tension at headquarters and a grimness that Charley had not sensed since that murderous night at Malvern Hill.

Jackson and his staff rode before the troops, weaving in

their saddles as they dozed. Once the General straightened himself. "Is that you, Charley?" he asked in a voice meant not to disturb the others.

"Why, yes sir," Charley answered, suddenly wide awake. The moon shed a soft blurred light that illumined the ghostly line of gray figures.

"You have no business here," the General said flatly. "You should be in school."

Charley gulped in surprise. "No sir, I mean—I. . . ."

"Your father would agree with me, wouldn't he—and your brother?" Jackson interrupted.

"Yes—yes sir," Charley admitted and rushed on. "But you see, I'm not a good student. I was taking a geometry exam when I ran away to join the army. I couldn't have passed it."

"Humph." It was a snort of disgust. "I was a schoolteacher before this war and I know from experience what a lad of your intelligence can learn. The effort is all that is lacking. Read your epigram, Charley."

There didn't seem to be an answer, or at least Charley couldn't think of one before the General slumped forward in his saddle and began to weave, quickly asleep. In the gray light of dawn the troops sank down in the streets of Sharpsburg to rest, and Jackson spurred away to rendezvous with Lee.

Artillery fire opened immediately, and by sunrise the battle tide was already high. Stonewall's men were placed at the left end of the Confederate forces, and the General was furious at the count—nearly forty per cent of his army was not present but straggling. There was little protection, only a whitewashed Dunkard church and a cornfield whose stalks stood taller than a man.

Charley rode beside Captain Douglas as the staff followed the General on inspection. The sun was blood-red, the artillery fire had already littered the ground with dead horses and broken equipment, and the singing of a shell was so near that Charley involuntarily crouched down against Pebbles' neck. Immediately he was humiliated. If anyone saw him they mustn't think that he was afraid.

He dismounted and took a bridle from a dead horse which he pretended to have been scrutinizing. "Thought this looked like a good bridle," he said loudly. "Pebbles is always slipping hers."

There was a humming sound like a stick being hurled through the air, an explosion not far away and something smacked Charley on the side, twirled him around and flattened him in the dirt. He saw bright lights burst in blackness and gasped painfully to fill his lungs with air. In an instant, Captain Douglas was there examining his body where his clothing was torn.

"You're not hurt, old man," Douglas said, helping him to a wobbly stance. "Just a fragment from that lamppost, as the boys call them. Or maybe it was a wash kettle—next time you'll know when to duck, eh?"

"Y–yes sir," Charley said, leaving the bridle on the ground.

"Here they come," someone shouted and all eyes turned towards the blue line that surged towards Stonewall's forces.

It was a hammer blow that battered the gray wall and beat holes in it in an incredibly short period. The Confederates regrouped barely in time to meet another charge and now half their number lay dead or wounded on the field. There was a desperate rally and a countercharge to a wild Rebel yell, but the blue line always had more men to fill its gaps and they came on like never-ending ocean waves.

"Private Randolph." It was Jackson, his eyes blazing with the fire of battle. "Carry a message to General Stuart." And the words were desperate. Stuart's troopers must stop the wounded who were leaving the front and keep them as reserves. Only unconsciousness or death freed a man from service today.

"Yes, sir." Charley rode until he found the chief of the cavalry with part of his horse artillery. As Jackson's line broke again, the troopers dismounted and fought on foot, their commander cheering them on. Stuart acted as if he thought it all a splendid rassle for his boys, his cinnamon beard bristling, plumed hat and French saber dancing in the sun. But when Charley gave him the message, even the jaunty cavalier was grim.

Back by the Dunkard church, the gray lines were so thin that it seemed they could only be playing at charging, falling back and regrouping. The cornfield had not a single stalk standing and the dead lay in rows among the stubble. Charley joined another messenger who was still panting from a frantic ride.

"There's no help fer it," the man muttered and threw himself onto the ground at the shriek of a shell close by. Calmly, he rose, already chewing his tobacco, and continued. "It don't take no general to see that if Stonewall don't run soon, they'll be no one who kin. Lawd, how them fellers fight!"

Woosh! The humming of a big stick flung through the air, and Charley hit the dirt with his companion. A "lamppost" dug itself into the ground in front of them and sprayed the earth into the air. Charley pressed his body flat and felt dirt raining down on top of him. It's like having my grave filled in on me, he thought.

"Now, that there one would-a kilt us," the man said. "Dad-shame I swallered my tobaccy."

But there was no time to marvel over their escape, for Charley was ordered to carry another message to Stuart as men maneuvered frantically to plug the gaping holes. Sometimes his duty took him far to the rear where stragglers came on doggedly, or hesitated, or tried to backtrack away from the battle.

"Hurry!" Charley yelled at them. "Are you turtles—or mules? Get to the front!"

"Listen to that goober pea poppin' off," one answered. "Shut up—you ain't nobody's boss."

The memory of the cornfield and its bloody harvest

flashed in Charley's mind. With one hand he dug out the lead balls from his pocket and put several in his mouth. He filled a derringer with powder, capped it and spat a ball down the barrel. "Now, git—you cowards," he shouted and circled Pebbles around them like cattle to be driven to the field. The first one to raise his musket received Charley's bullet through his hat.

"You fire-eatin' hornet," a man cried, but Charley crowded him with Pebbles and whacked him across the head with the butt of his pistol. He turned to the third, pouring powder again and spitting in the ball, but the man was already running toward the front, and Charley placed his bullet at the heels of any who hesitated.

Captain Douglas pounded down the road on a fresh horse. He doffed his hat to Charley and cried, "Good hunting," as he dashed by.

It was only noontime. Charley was riding beside the General once again and the Yanks had ceased their blows at the Dunkard church. Almost at its last gasp, Stonewall's unit had been left to pick up its shattered remnants while the enemy hurled itself at the center of Lee's line. It was hot and Charley looked up at the fiery sun and wondered if it had stopped moving across the sky.

The afternoon was more terrible than the morning. He saw the dead piled fifteen feet deep in the sunken road at the center of the line. Then the enemy pressure was taken from there and thrown at the right end of the Confederates and battle was joined as if it were a new dawn. Charley's head swam with fatigue and he snatched moments of sleep in the saddle. Jackson sat on his horse, sending and receiving messengers calmly, but his eyes seemed as sharp as the points of bayonets.

"Randolph." It was the General's voice, dry as salt. "Find General Early. Tell the General to press the enemy in the rear and towards the river."

Charley obeyed instantly, but his wits were dull and he rode into such a storm of firing that he doubted he would live to ride out of it. Shot, shells, canister, bullets and balls, so thick that he could almost see them, ripped and shrieked around his head. If God would let him live through this, there must be something in the world for him to do other than war.

It was a miracle, he thought as he passed out of the firing and delivered the message. Afterwards he laughed hysterically; little Charley Randolph had been telling the generals what to do all day. Now he sought out stragglers who were crowding in as a regular command of fresh troops hurried to the front behind them.

It was real help! Help—if it weren't too late. Sharpsburg was in flames and flocks of bewildered pigeons wheeled above its smoking roofs. Yanks had crossed Antietam Creek and the southern cause was ready to be crushed on this hideous field.

Charley stampeded Pebbles into the midst of stragglers, yelling, clubbing and firing his pistols.

The soldiers cursed him as everything small and loathsome, but he didn't care. "Fools! Cowards!" he raged, and drove them up the road.

Was that the same sun in the sky? Charley moaned, conscious of his aching body and bruised side. How could the Army of Northern Virginia endure another moment?

And yet, it did. With fresh troops and new hope, Charley saw the boys in rags leap forward over Union dead, screaming the Rebel yell and the fox-hunter's call. He saw the blue line sag and fall back. Guns on the heights bellowed to a roar of triumph and he himself galloped like a crazy man with new messages for generals on the offensive.

At last, nightfall came on the longest day in the lives of a hundred thousand men. A fifth were dead or wounded and the rest spent a horrible, rain-soaked night snatching at sleep or plodding through puddles of blood and water to find a buddy or help the wounded.

Even the General had no tent, and headquarters was a grassy place under a tree. In the morning, the sun rose to sparkle on the raindrops. Bullet-tattered leaves flapped like tiny banners in the breeze. General Stuart rode in singing, "Jine the Cavalry," the tassels of his gold sash swinging merrily. Captain Douglas jumped to welcome him, as Charley sat up on the ground where he had fallen asleep.

"Ho! There you are," General Stuart said, pointing to Charley. "As fine a courier as ever wore the gray— and I shall tell General Jackson so, and write you up in my report. What's your name, lad?"

Charley sprang to his feet and saluted, and Captain Douglas answered for him.

"Charles Randolph, sir," Douglas said. "You should have seen him driving in stragglers yesterday—he was all over a dozen of them, routing them like a one-man army."

The officers shouted with laughter and Charley grinned, still sleepy. "We won, didn't we?" he asked.

The question seemed to take the fun out of Captain Douglas but General Stuart bellowed assurance. "Of course we won—it was a great victory. Oh, I tell you, Randolph, every fighting man in our army is a hero today."

An hour later, Jackson ordered Charley to ride with him and the staff to meet General Lee. Burial parties and ambulances were everywhere but for the unharmed it was a beautiful, blessed day. If the General was not jubilant, he seemed grimly satisfied and praised God for goodness and mercy to his forces. Perhaps it was relief from the pressure of yesterday, but the staff rode gaily and some-one mentioned that the birds were singing. Charley's spirits rose. Hadn't Jackson been content to have him called his son? Hadn't Stuart and Douglas praised him? The agony of yesterday had already passed into history.

Jackson and Lee talked privately and then rode back to the waiting party.

"And this is he," General Jackson was saying. "A cousin of yours, he tells me, from Warrenton."

Why, he means me, Charley thought. Excitement

welled up in him as if all the bugles in the world were sounding the attack. What were the two generals saying about him?

General Lee's smile was warm and he nodded his head slightly to Charley as Jackson continued. "We want you to know of his gallantry in driving in stragglers and his good service in carrying messages during extreme personal peril."

Charley flushed and looked down at the ground to hide his riotous, joyous confusion. Captain Douglas and the others were there to see him in conversation with General Robert E. Lee but he was too overwhelmed to say a word.

He looked up, grinning like a foolish schoolboy, as his Commanding General bowed gravely to him. "I am indeed proud that my young kinsman has merited such commendation."

"Ho!" Charley said under his breath and felt his face burning with blushes.

"Thank you, sir," he stuttered at last as the generals turned to other business and members of the staff gathered around to congratulate him.

This was fame! This was exaltation beyond anything he had ever known; the air he breathed seemed scarlet and golden. This was his Victory!

Glory, glory, glory!

16 The White and Gold

THE ARMY withdrew from Maryland into the great Valley of Virginia. Here was the breadbasket of the South; its natural fruitfulness was hardly damaged although war had harvested too many of its young men. The corn shocks stood like ten thousand tepees in mile after mile of cultivated fields and the pumpkins lay fat and wobbly on their sides. Virginia creeper traced streaks of scarlet up dark tree trunks; sumac and sassafras burned like fire in the sunlight. There were walnuts and chestnuts, turnips and onions, fish and quail, eggs and milk. Camping here, Charley fared well, as a slow autumn passed into December and the army fought at Fredericksburg and settled into winter quarters.

New boots came from Unc Ben at last and Charley pulled them on proudly. "Look, General," he said, slapping the polished leather. "Now I'm really ready to go to war."

"They'll do very well," the General said. "But you won't need them for war. I'm going to write a letter of recommendation to Virginia Military Institute for you. You'll be able to enroll in several weeks at mid-term."

"No, General," Charley cried. "I mean, thank you, sir,

but I don't want to go to school. With Father in prison and The Grove burned, there isn't anything important but fighting and . . . and being your courier. . . ."

Jackson ignored the outburst. "You'll find V.M.I. a fine opportunity to complete your education. I had the honor of being a member of its faculty before the war. There are many spirited young men your own age. . . ."

"Boys!" Charley said with contempt. He saw the General's expression harden, but he kept on. "No sir, thank you, but I won't trouble you to write that letter."

"It's officer's training school," Jackson said dryly. "Surely you hope to rise above the rank of private."

"Oh, not especially. I like being a courier." Charley knew he sounded like a child pleading for candy. "I just want to stay. . . ."

General Jackson's blue eyes flashed. "Those are my orders, Private Randolph, and I expect you to carry them out."

Orders to go to school! Jackson could have asked him to capture Washington and he would gladly have tried. But this was too hard—too humiliating. Charley bit his lip; when a good soldier had orders, there was only one thing to do.

Another week passed, and he held in his hand an honorable discharge from the Army of Northern Virginia. There were only brief, jolly-sounding farewells to Captain Douglas and Robert, though he was too sick inside to look them squarely in the eyes. They clapped him on the back and said what a fine opportunity this was and what fun he'd have with the cadets. Cock-and-bull stories! If only they wouldn't send him away.

"General Jackson, sir," Charley said that same afternoon. "I've come to say goodbye."

The General was busy with dispatches and there was already a courier to replace Charley. "Glad you stopped. If you apply yourself at V.M.I. the way you have here, you'll have no trouble."

"Yes sir." Charley waited until Jackson finished scribbling a message and then asked, "When I'm graduated— and an officer—could I come back with you?"

The General put down his quill and came to clasp Charley's hand. "Of course. If it's God's will. A man doesn't forget such loyalty as yours. Good luck."

Charley saluted and hurried away. He felt tears welling up in his eyes and it wasn't something that a modern Joshua—a greater than Napoleon—should see in Charley Randolph, veteran. There was nothing to do now but take Pebbles to Unc Ben and head for the school at Lexington.

Charley stood at parade rest beneath the dun-colored towers of V.M.I. It was hot, as hot as the May day he had galloped from The Grove a year ago. Six months since he'd seen General Jackson, four months here eating growley day in and day out, sitting in dull battered classrooms with a bunch of boys in monkey suits. Tender green grass fringed the base of the grim buildings, and House Mountain rose beyond in full foliage, but nothing softened the demands of the school. Books—demerits!

Charley shifted his position and sighed. There were rules about everything: eating, sleeping, coming, going, how long the gaslights could burn, how much water could be drawn into his pail from the school hydrant. *Analytic Geometry* weighed more in hand than his derringers. There was only one place of refuge to remember the battles and the glory and the awfulness too—in Stonewall's former classroom, where it was quiet and chapel-like.

"Parade dismissed," came the order and Charley snorted to himself. The cadet officer's voice sounded like a banty rooster straining to crow; this was his captain who had never seen a battle nor a Yank. And he, whom the boys called Little General, was a private, Company C, a member of the fifth form, lower than the low.

As they broke formation, Charley looked around for his buddies, Sam and Moses. "Wait," he called, but a little boy, from the group of townsfolk who came to watch the drill, darted forward and thrust a note into his hand. The messenger ran away instantly and Charley opened the paper.

Meet me on the square rite away.

A Front Royal Soldier.

"Hey, Sam, look at this." He trotted after his friend and showed him the note.

"You can't leave campus now," Sam said. "You're going to get in trouble."

"Not if you help me." Charley felt the first thrill of real excitement since his battlefield days. "Come on, Sam, be a sport. I've got to find out about it."

"Well...."

"Look, I saved a blank from practice." Charley dug in his pocket for the cartridge. "All you gotta do is fire it off towards town if that old drum starts rolling muster. They won't know who did it."

Sam nodded. "But you got to run like the cavalry to get back here before that drum stops beating. You know that."

"Don't worry. I'm not taking any chances. I wouldn't want to face General Jackson again if I got kicked out of V.M.I." Charley saw how easily he could use the cover of trees and walls to get him away from school and into Lexington.

"Hunh," Sam said. "With all your demerits, they got you half crated for shipping already. And say, did you hear that Stonewall was wounded?"

"Sure, I heard it," Charley said and shrugged. "Rumors—soldier-talk. Nothing could ever hurt him, not Joshua."

Sam looked puzzled, but Charley was on his way, soon

out of sight of school and running openly down the sidewalks of town. He recognized a faculty officer coming from the opposite direction, and vaulted the hedge into a private yard, following the garden fence to safety. He spotted his soldier on the deserted square and rushed up to him. "Here I am. Charles Randolph. But we can't stand here. We got to get back towards school so I can make formation in a hurry. . . ."

The soldier loped along beside Charley. "Don't you git me in no officer's nest," he said. "I'm kinda extendin' my leave on my own say so I could git here atall."

"Not looking for officers myself," Charley said as he led the way into a wooded place next to school property. "Now—what's this about? Is it Mrs. Bly or word from Warrenton, or. . . ."

"My—ain't you a little girl's purty!" The soldier was surveying him with a taunting smile and Charley looked down at his spotless uniform with gold buttons and his fine boots with only a haze of parade-ground dust on last night's shine.

He glanced at the soldier's raggedness and flushed. "Aw, they're only monkey suits," he said. "But quick, what's. . . ."

"Leetle and lively as ginger, that's the way Mary said you was," the soldier began. "Mary Bly and me is kin. I was a-visitin' her when the Yanks come in sudden-like and she sent me packin' into the mountains to hide. Old feller, name of Quinton Hocks."

"Yes, how is he?" Charley watched the faculty member come in from town, glancing from side to side, looking for an unidentified cadet who disappeared over someone's hedge.

"He ain't good," the soldier said. "When I got to his cabin, thar he lay on the ground with a bullet in his back. I nursed him all night. . . ."

"Shot in the back?" Charley cried. "Who'd do a murdering, sneaking trick like that?"

"His neighbors done it fer heppin' darkies to get North. Oh, he was crazy out of his head mos' of the time, but long towards mornin' he talked plain. He said he owed you fer a hoss and made me take out loose stones in the fireplace to get you money. You know what I found?"

"No." Charley stared at the man trying to anticipate his words.

"Jist another rock! This here one. He asked me to keep it in my pocket til I found you. Waal, he was a-dyin' thar, so I promised." He placed a rag-tied lump in the palm of Charley's hand.

"But you said he was dying." Charley's words were strangled.

"Yep, he died. Out of his senses and a-ravin' that no one would ever find his silver mine. Kin you imagine a crazy old beggar like that thinkin' he was rich?"

Somewhere within the V.M.I. garrison, a shot sounded and the first beat of the muster roll began its urgent message.

167

"Thanks," Charley said and grabbed the man's hand in a warm clasp. He knew tears were running down his cheeks as he turned and raced for the rear of the school.

But the soldier called after him, "They're a-sayin' Stonewall's done fer—you 'spose it's true?"

"No!" Charley screamed as he ran. "No. No. No."

He pounded across the campus, through the halls and as the last of the drum roll sounded, took his place in the cadet formation. His breathing was loud and rasping, his eyes stung and his face burned—yet he stood at rigid attention while the officers checked and reported all present and accounted for.

As the group disbanded, Sam came up to him with their friend Moses. "What was it?" Sam asked. "Say, have you been crying?"

"No," Charley said. "Of course not. It wasn't anything, only this." His hand relaxed its cramped clutch on the stone and Sam tore away the rag. It was a rough, black chunk, flaky and soft-feeling for a rock.

Sam and Moses looked questioningly at Charley. "Could be an ore," Charley said lamely.

Moses motioned towards a faculty officer. "He teaches geology—let's ask him.

"Captain, sir," he called and saluted. "Will you tell us what this is?"

The Captain nodded and Charley handed him the rock. "Umm—exceptional—high silver content. See, this rock is black because of the tarnish on the silver." He scraped the surface with his thumbnail and a silvery-white color was underneath. "Where'd you get it?"

Charley took the rock and held it tightly in his hand. "It was willed to me," he said. "I don't feel so well, sir. I got to go."

He saluted and ran towards his room as he heard the Captain say, "Was Randolph crying?"

"No sir," Sam's reply followed, "of course not."

Charley went to the barracks room he shared with four roommates, found a lemon he had put in his drawer yesterday, and walked slowly to the classroom where General Jackson used to teach. It seemed deserted and Charley seated himself on the edge of a chair, booted toes pointing rigidly straight ahead. He cut a hole in the lemon with his penknife and felt its acid juice in his mouth. This was the way Stonewall had sat in front of headquarters tent on many occasions. Stonewall could not be dead—lesser men like poor old Quint. . . .

"Er—Randolph."

"Yes sir." Charley jumped up and saluted. It was Captain Preston, a veteran like himself, who had lost an arm in battle.

"It's about your work, Private Randolph," the Captain said, seating himself and motioning for Charley to do the same. "You're on the verge—what will you do if you flunk out?"

"I'll go to the front, sir. Maybe I can persuade General Jackson to take me back," Charley said, though he didn't really believe it. He plunged on. "And after that I'll . . . I'll be a mercenary soldier and fight anywhere in the world and get paid for it too."

Captain Preston remained silent for a moment and then spoke softly. "But Charley, war is death, suffering, mutilation." He made the smallest gesture towards his empty sleeve.

"You don't understand!" Charley jumped up in confusion. "I mean that war's exciting—it's . . . well, it makes you feel as big as a giant. You should see the General's eyes flash when the battle is toughest . . . and. . . ."

"Randolph," Captain Preston interrupted. "I have some very bad news for you. General Jackson is dead."

"Dead?" Charley repeated and the officer nodded.

"No," he cried wildly. "Wounded maybe, but the Yanks can't kill him. They can't! I know that."

"The Yanks didn't—our own men shot him by mistake." Captain Preston emphasized each word. "War killed Jackson—remember that. War killed him."

Charley closed his eyes and shuddered as memory turned crazily in his head. It was black night in the deafening roar of battle. A shell exploded in his brain and shrapnel tore holes in his side. He slumped to the chair, sobbing. "Oh God, You wouldn't let it happen to Joshua. It isn't true. I won't believe it."

But two days later, the remains of General Jackson lay in state in his old classroom, and Charley took his turn as honor guard for the dead. He had fought the knowledge of this truth until emotion was exhausted, and now he looked before him with dull tearless eyes. The room was draped in black, banked with flowers. Governors and generals filed past the casket in tribute; outside, the beautiful white-and-gold flag of V.M.I. sagged at half mast and Virginia, the South, sank down in grief. Stonewall was dead; Stonewall had been mortal like other men.

Numbly, Charley followed the funeral procession to the open grave in Lexington and watched the last rites. Somehow the benediction was for humble old Quint as well as for his General. War had killed them both, yet nothing remained but war.

Sudden fear welled up in Charley. He must have something to cling to. He clutched at his breast pocket and felt the epigram crumple against his body. General Lee had smiled and praised him once. What was it the epigram said?

A foe may give lessons in fighting, but life teaches learning.

17 Go in with a Cheer

CHARLEY walked with his friend Moses toward the limits-gate, a path he had taken a hundred times since Jackson's death. "I can go out that gate for good if I want," Charley said. "There's still Robert. He'd be as mad as a battery of howitzers, but I could join him in Richmond."

Moses shrugged. "When old Stonewall was alive, you might have done it, but not now. It's a point of honor, I guess."

"That's not fair! It's been over a year already!" Charley turned on his friend, emotion quivering in his voice. "We're losing the war now that Jackson's gone, you know that, don't you? They need everybody at the front, even half-pints like me. . . ."

"Aww—forget it, Little General," Moses said, and leaned against the limits-gate, scowling.

The evening gun boomed and Charley turned to watch the garrison flag sink slowly from its peak on the barracks tower. He had dutifully kept at his studies all this time as his memorial to Stonewall, but it was no good. He could find no interest in books except those of the General's which still lined the shelves in his old classroom.

They were difficult texts on religion and mostly too hard to understand, but he liked to flip through the pages for the comfort of being close to Stonewall's world. Occasionally, a new thought made him sit up eagerly on the edge of his chair, his mind stampeding through the pages with all the fervor he had felt when herding the stragglers in Maryland. Here was Jackson's God.

He tried to tell Moses about it. "Stonewall always said it was God who won his victories, and we used to have to wait outside his tent while he finished morning devotions. He was a lot like a minister."

"Oh, I see what you're thinking," Moses said, surveying him. "You've decided to be a preacher, but you sure as the devil don't look like one."

Charley grinned. Let Moses think what he would, but Jackson's courier had never considered that before. He had given everything to war relief, his chunk of silver ore, even his extra underclothes to be torn up for bandages, everything but Lee's epigram—which could have been auctioned at a benefit bazaar. Jackson had said Charley didn't understand it, so he'd keep it until he did.

Moses was halfway back to the barracks. "Come on, Little General," he yelled, and Charley trailed after him. There was something fine about V.M.I., but Captain Preston knew he intended to leave in June. It was hard to know where Stonewall would have ordered him, now that volunteers were so desperately needed.

In the middle of that same Tuesday night, the drum

sounded the long roll.   Charley struggled out of his bunk, pulled on his trousers sleepily and ran barefooted toward the cadet formation near Washington's statue.

"What's this about?" he yelled to Moses.

"Fire drill, I guess," Moses answered.

"Naw," Sam grumbled.   "Probably some of the faculty saw one of the guys down town."

But the drum made chills run up Charley's back as he took his place in the lines.   It was persistent, strong, throbbing with excitement—nothing routine or petty could follow a sound like that.   Officers scanned a paper by lantern light, their faces made grotesque by the shadows, and the adjutant began to read the orders.   Charley stood at parade rest with his heart thumping against his ribs.   The corps listened in absolute silence as the various voices gave them directions.   "March to war at dawn," the adjutant said.   The first sergeant told them, "Bring canteens, haversacks and blankets at 4 A.M."   Then someone snapped, "Parade dismissed," and company after company broke ranks, cheering and stampeding through the corridors to make ready.   They breakfasted by candlelight and filled the haversacks from the messhall tables.

"Only hardtack and bacon, boys," Charley called to his friends, and they chose as he directed, leaving the perishables for the less experienced.

Charley felt a twinge of pride.   The cadets were watching him now, taking their cues from his every action.   The corps hiked up the road in the spirit of boys going to a picnic. People came from their houses to cheer and throw May flowers, and there was a dance in their honor in Staunton the next night. The following day, they tramped up the Valley pike singing, but by afternoon they began to tire and refugees from war passed them going south.

"Sigel," passed the chilling word. "Yankee General Sigel was at Strasburg in heavy force. He was moving down on Confederate General Breckenridge. You'll meet Breckenridge this evening. Hurry."

It began to rain and the cadets' spirits sank heavily to the sodden earth. Camp was almost silent that night as Charley sat with his friends. "Want me to tell you about Port Republic?" he asked, but no one murmured to hear that story again. "Well, how about Second Manassas and the greatest feast in history?" This usually brought a yell of approval from the hearers, but now there was no response. Charley's falsely cheerful voice grated on his own nerves, but he decided to try the sure cure for depression and the cadets sang dutifully:

> Oh, I wish I was in the Land of Cotton.
> Old times there are not forgotten.
> Look away, look away,
> Look away, Dixie land.

A cadet messenger from Captain Preston burst into their midst. "Hey, Little General, there was a courier at headquarters to see you. He'd been riding all day—big battle down around Richmond yesterday."

"Robert!" Charley sprang forward and dashed into the black, rain-drenched night. The messenger followed, sloshing behind him towards headquarters tent. "Was he from my brother?" Charley asked, feeling the raindrops hit his face and roll down his cheeks.

"I don't know," the boy answered, panting. "All I know was that Captain Preston didn't want to tell you . . . the messenger made him promise . . . said it was orders from Douglas or somebody."

And now it was certain that Robert too had been killed. Charley stopped running and walked doggedly in and saluted Captain Preston. He hardly heard as the officer told him what he already sensed—Robert had fallen with a mortal wound.

"Was there anything else?" Charley asked numbly, staring at the Captain's empty sleeve. He didn't expect any answer, but he had to say something.

"Jeb Stuart," Preston said quietly. "For all his plumed hat and gold sash—he too is gone. Don't let the boys know; there's no strength for them in that."

Charley brushed his hand over the epigram in his pocket. "We could lose this war, couldn't we, sir? General Lee can't fight it alone—so many of his best men are dead now."

"Peace will come," Captain Preston said. "And some of you boys will not know what to do with yourselves."

Charley saluted and turned to leave.

"Randolph," Captain Preston said. "I want you in my class again—when there's peace."

"I don't know, sir," Charley muttered, suddenly gasping to control the swelling sobs in his throat. "Maybe."

The next day, the cadet corps marched grimly up the Valley, joining now with the Virginia veterans. Charley kept his tragic news to himself, mulling it in his mind as his feet sloshed in the mud. Why had God let Robert and the others be killed? When he got back to school he'd search through Jackson's books. He sighed. It took a lot of learning to be a general—a preacher—or even to return to The Grove and make a going farm of it.

Ho! That's what Jackson wanted him to understand about the epigram—"life teaches learning."

"Lawdee," a ragged old-timer drawled at the cadets. "Now what's them leetle fellers thar?"

"Toy so'jurs," his shoeless buddy said. "The Lawd done blowed breath into some toy so'jurs and sent 'em here to hep us."

There was a shout of laughter from the veterans and Charley smiled at their familiar brand of humor.

"I'll show you if we're toys!" Sam jumped forward, fists doubled and face flushed with anger.

Charley glanced around and was amazed to see the whole corps seething with injured pride. "Why you grizzled old bears," Charley shouted back, "you haven't seen a good army in so long you don't know one in front of your nose."

The Johnny Rebs grinned and let it go at that for the moment. But soon a chorus of "Rock-a-Bye Baby" plagued the cadets' march. Charley laughed and shrugged and the boys did their best to follow suit.

There were reports of enemy scouts now and everyone realized that tomorrow the battle would be joined. The boys went into camp early and Charley wandered away by himself, glad of a chance to relax his cheerful manner. Poor kids, he thought as he trudged up a ridge to view the Valley, they have so much to learn. Learn—there it was again . . . "life teaches learning." Charley's doubts faded as his gaze swept the crest of the familiar mountain. Yes, he wanted to return to V.M.I.

Suddenly he saw a surge of movement from the corner of his eye and he jumped behind a tree trunk. Across on a smaller ridge an enemy horseman had appeared, a scout on a magnificent horse. Charley looked again, cautiously peering while the hair prickled on the back of his neck. Sun Bolt! The Spirit of Victory ridden by a burly Yank. Sun Bolt meant death. Quint Junior had cursed him with that. The rider whirled and disappeared toward his own lines, and Charley began to shake with fear. There's nothing to it, he told himself as he ran stumbling back to camp.

"There's nothing to it!" he said again and again, but his foot caught on a root and he sprawled on the ground. He lay there, his face on the wet grass. "God—if you'll save me—I'll make it up to You somehow." It was a long while before he found the inner strength to rise and rejoin the cadets, acting as if nothing had happened. That night they received their issue of ammunition, forty cartridges to each soldier for his muzzle-loader.

At one o'clock in the rain-drenched morning, the boys were quietly awakened; they held prayer service, cooked rations and marched at dawn towards New Market. Charley felt his friends' nervous glances; he saw how they were watching him, how they seemed to lean on his banter—as strained and false as it must sound.

"Rock-a-bye baby," the veterans taunted them, rocking their arms cradlelike and grinning, and the cadets returned the grin.

They are learning, Charley thought, and so am I. He looked down at his boots carrying him step by step to battle, new boots by the war's standard though the same Unc Ben had sent him. The individual roar of the big guns could be heard up ahead, and they were ordered to lay aside blanket rolls to be free for action. Two hundred twenty-five boys obeyed, some with an exaggerated flourish, some with trembling hands. Charley's own palms were drenched with sweat and his throat too dry to swallow. If only he hadn't seen Sun Bolt his old confidence might return, and the feeling of glory—if only he hadn't looked straight at the cursed horse.

"Well, this is it," Moses said in a low voice. "I'm not going to run, but I'm going to duck every chance I get."

He laughed quaveringly. "Promise to look me up if I don't report at roll call tonight. Will you promise me, Charley?"

"Yes," Charley said. "And you look for me too. Don't leave New Market until you know what happened to me." They shook hands and Charley glanced at the other cadets exchanging vows.

"Well, Little General, what do you say?" one of the boys called.

Charley stood tall and brandished an imaginary officer's saber. "I say let's go in with a cheer." His voice rang with an exaltation he could not feel.

There was a shout of assent that was soon drowned under the crash of cannonading. The corps moved forward through the streets of New Market and saw plainly the Federal guns on the ridges to the north. Between the two forces was a sloping plateau, with tall grass, cedars, an orchard, rail and stone fences. The mountains stood serene and aloof in soft spring foliage; new wheat blades bent under the feet of young soldiers. The valley mud sucked at their shoes as if to keep them from the attack, but each delay was followed by a sure advance.

Charley walked proudly though inwardly he was on his knees to Jackson's God: he saw Sam glance at him and straightened his sagging shoulders. They joined an outfit of veterans whose purpose was to capture a Yankee battery and a section of infantry. There'd be a charge across that long gully-ripped field, up that ridge with canister pouring down on top of them. The boys' pink faces had blanched white, but all eyes were straight ahead; every jaw was clamped in determination. Captain Preston led them with Major Shipp. It was past noon; the order to charge would come in minutes.

Save me, Charley prayed. Save us all. If I live, it'll be like Robert would want me to—and Stonewall.

"Charge!" came the command, almost lost in the Rebel yell that broke from every throat. The corps jumped forward, unable to bear the straining inactivity another instant. They marched into direct fire in perfect formation, just as on the parade ground at Lexington. Every voice continued to shout in relief to be moving, to encourage comrades, to damn the enemy. Up and down the gullies they went, past the cedars to the orchard, under increasing fire with boys dropping on every side. Suddenly, only four hundred yards ahead, blue infantry rose in front of the Yank battery, and the command came to halt and fix bayonets under a rain of shells and bullets. An explosion knocked Major Shipp off his feet, but he jumped up immediately. Another shell whistled by and Moses dived against the ground, rising quickly but not abashed.

Charley had become suddenly calm, with only one thought—advance as fast as possible and wipe out that murderous battery. "Come on," he yelled at Moses, actually smiling as his friend wiped the mud from his eyes. "There's no use dodging, boys. If a ball's going to hit you, it'll hit you anyway."

The order now was to advance on the double-quick; shoulder to shoulder the corps sprinted forward for the final plunge.

There was an ear-splitting noise, lightning flashed in Charley's mind, and a blow that was all the fury of war smashed into him. He was reeling—falling, falling into blackness.

From some deep abyss, Charley's consciousness clung and crawled up towards the light of life. Something jerked him and his head was run through with pain; flashes of light stabbed at his eyes though his lids were closed. He wanted to cry out but he could not; his body lay limp and useless around the spark of his mind.

Voices. Far away it seemed. Faintly heard through the thunder in his head.

"Poor mite," a man drawled. "Don't look a day past thirteen—a-layin' thar all bloody and dead."

"Fought like devils, them leetle fellers—better'n a full-growed man," someone answered. There was another jerk and Charley realized they were taking his boots from his legs.

"He won't need these no more," the first voice said, fading now. A scene from his memory took form in Charley's tottering consciousness. Quint Junior bent over the dead Yank, robbing him of his boots. He, on Pebbles, charged the thief in red fury. But that was long ago. Now, he wondered vaguely if there were feet small enough among the barefoot Johnny Rebs to wear his boots; he hoped so.

He could feel the blackness seeping around his mind again. They thought he was dead, those fellow soldiers whose voices he could not hear any more but somehow still felt their presence around him. He must give them a sign so that the ambulance wagon would carry him to the surgeon, or they might leave him here to be buried on the field.

Charley made an effort to call out. He reached down into the depth of his physical strength and silently cried out to God. A few hours ago his voice had carried to his comrades above the rattle of musketry; a few hours ago, the Rebel yell had come loud and lustily from his throat. But now he wasn't sure if an eyelid flicked or if his lips twitched a bit. He could do no more. Consciousness reeled through banks of fog and his thoughts were blotted out.

"Charley! Charley, can your hear me?" It was Moses' voice. Was Moses dead too—were they both in glory together? Or . . . or. . . . Slowly he opened his eyes, feeling the light of life brighten the darkness. Moses was there, standing beside him, grinning and crying and choking out words.

"You're all right," Moses was saying. "You're in the hospital—you're going to get well—not for a long time maybe, but you will, you will."

Charley looked at him, trying to smile. He realized his

head was bandaged except for one side of his face. Carefully he moved his arms and legs just enough to know he was whole.

Moses was talking more easily now. "We captured the battery all right. The Yanks left New Market and chased back up the Valley. There are about fifty of our boys here in the hospital and around town. Captain Preston'll be in to see you." Moses pressed his hand. "I got to go now."

Closing his eyes, Charley felt his strength collecting like dew, unseen, from nowhere, but real. They must have given him morphine because the pain was not severe. He was alive! Sun Bolt had failed! He had his whole life to live.

Sometime, many misty hours later, Captain Preston came to his bedside with a nurse.

"He must have been one of the boys the women carried from the field," she was saying. "He's no bigger than a child."

"Ah, no," Captain Preston said, taking Charley's hand and looking into his face. "Big—as big as his General. Big as Stonewall himself."

Charley smiled. "Captain," he formed the words painfully. "Enroll me in your class. I want to come."

"Of course." The officer's face lighted happily. "I thought you would."

"Paper in my pocket . . . please," Charley mumbled,

and the nurse searched through his clothes until she found the epigram.

"Here," Charley motioned to Preston. "You could sell it for war relief. I don't need it any more."

Charley closed his eyes as the visitors moved away. He'd been a good courier, but now he must think of the long life ahead. Maybe he was being too big for his britches again, but he could learn to make a good job of this too . . . for the sake of all his dead.

Charley turned his thoughts to Stonewall and prayed for peace.

About the Author

THE BEAUTIFUL Shenandoah Valley which we glimpse in STONE-WALL'S COURIER is well known to Virginia Hinkins. She was born in Baltimore, Maryland, and resided for some years in Front Royal, Virginia, with her husband, Dr. John F. Cadden.

As a student in a young ladies' prep school, she developed a love for horseback riding, and this enthusiasm led her to becoming a bona fide farmer at nineteen. After graduating from Pennsylvania School of Horticulture for Women, she devoted twelve years to managing Spengler Hall in Strasburg, Virginia. Built by her father's great-great grandfather in 1805–1810, Spengler Hall at that time included "all the land from mountain to mountain." But writing has always absorbed Virginia Hinkins's interest, and before she ever undertook a junior novel she served as contributing editor of a monthly farm paper.

STONEWALL'S COURIER is based on fact. Charles Randolph really did become Jackson's courier after he picked up the General's glove at Port Republic. The records tell of Jackson's commendations of Charley to Lee and General Stuart's written reports in his praise. The Randolph family has his honorable discharge from the Army, and Virginia Military Institute the records of his attendance there as a student sent by Jackson. We know too that when he was grown he became a minister. Miss Hinkins has had access to family records in writing this book, and a member of the Randolph family has read the story chapter by chapter.

If you enjoyed
STONEWALL'S COURIER . . . then you will want to know about some other books from Loft Press:

THOMAS JEFFERSON TREATS HIMSELF . . . A fascinating and compelling look at an everyday aspect of one of the world's best-known, most studied historical personalities. The reader sees Jefferson, the man, engaged in the fight for good health, and under such conditions as *modern* man can hardly envision. Jefferson developed an understanding of preventive health mainten-ance far ahead of his time. Combining exercise, diet, and observation, he devised a holistic regi-men of daily health care. He was determined to stay physically and mentally healthy and, as much as possible, away from the doctor. By John M. Holmes, Ph.D.

THE GAME OF SCHOOL . . . In all the cacaph-ony about schools, the voices of classroom teach-ers and students are seldom heard. In a bracing departure from most education books, author Robert L. Tripp includes student voices. His ideas for reform—fresh, relevant, and experi-ence-based—brightly contrast with the sleepy

(continued overleaf)

conventional theories that pour out of educational commissions and task forces. Tripp, a realist and a radical, makes the very basic point that education must involve students. It should give them the tools—and the inclination—to use reason, not just rote memory. A must book for those interested in the education of our youth.

POETRY FROM THE VALLEY OF VIRGINIA . . .
A delightful anthology of contemporary poetry from and about the great Shenandoah Valley of Virginia. Poetry from the preoccupied to the profound, from light to sturdy, some throat-catching, some belly-laughing, and mixes of all these characteristics. The results of the biennial competitions sponsored by Loft Press, *Poetry from the Valley of Virginia* is a snapshot of current poetical impulse in this historic region.

To order or enquire about other titles available contact
Loft Press at P.O. Box 126, Fort Valley, VA 22652